WIND, WATER ROCK AND SKY

THE STORY OF COGNASHENE, GEORGIAN BAY

THE COGNASHENE BOOK CORPORATION, 1997

ISBN 0-9681895-0-4
Published by The Cognashene Book Corporation
Copyright © 1997 The Cognashene Book Corporation
Edited by Jennifer David
Design and Art Direction by Carol Moskot
Cover photograph and endpaper courtesy of The Charles McGibbon Family
Back cover photograph by Dick Cutler
Printed in Canada by Friesens Printing
No portion of this book may be reproduced without the permission of
The Cognashene Book Corporation
First Edition

CONTENTS

FOREWORD

THERE'S SOMETHING unique about belonging to the community that is Cognashene. Having spent sixty-seven years cottaging among its breathtakingly beautiful islands, I take tremendous pride in its history, and at the same time feel a strong sense of responsibility regarding its future.

As a refuge from the vagaries of city life, Cognashene is irreplaceable in the lives of all its inhabitants. Never was this more apparent to me than during my years in the political arena, when time spent on the Bay was a true tonic, a time of rest, renewal and often, introspection. I've sometimes wondered if there isn't some restorative power in the bracing Georgian Bay air.

Certainly there is some benefit in being surrounded—and distracted—by the wild and temperamental nature of the Bay. It is, to my mind, an unsurpassable sensation, though having said that, it is just as much the warmth, kindness and tremendous community spirit of family and friends that continue to draw us back, year after year.

This book is a testament to that spirit. More than just a written and visual chronicle of the area, *Wind, Water, Rock and Sky* paints a vivid picture of the colourful character and appeal of Cognashene, and just as importantly it recalls the people and places that belong to this distinctive island community. Moreover, it lends some insight into the early development of southern Ontario and the adventurous pioneers who helped to tame it.

As with many precious things, it can be all too easy to take a special place like Cognashene for granted. But for those of us who live here and for those with whom we share this glorious part of the Bay there remains an important obligation. We have a responsibility to ensure that steps are taken to protect the environment, water quality, traditions and values of the place we call home first, and Cognashene second.

This is never an easy task in the face of growth and change, but with our collective commitment and respect, Cognashene as we know and cherish it will endure for generations to come.

— THE HON. WILLIAM G. DAVIS

INTRODUCTION

THIS BOOK IS A CELEBRA-tion in words and pictures of a very particular part of the world: the Cogna-shene area of Georgian Bay.

Wind, water, and sky are familiar features of a great many places on earth. It is the rocks of the Great Canadian Shield, however, that dom-inate the particular land and water-scape of Georgian Bay and, in combi-nation with the winds, the waters and the skies, transform Cognashene into something unique and powerful. Together they conjure in the mind's eye images which illuminate many of the lesser days of the year when the seasonal population is living apart from Cognashene and regretting the lengthy separation.

not immediately discernible, and where a sense of the immutability of the rocks and the pines transcends the mundane and creates an irrefutable link between the self and the universe.

The writer E. M. Forster encour-aged us to "only connect." Within this book lie many opportunities to connect with Cognashene, with its geography, topography, geology, with its unyielding rocks, its deceptive calm, its abrupt and violent storms, its mesmerizing sunsets, and above all, with generations of people whose lives have been enriched by it in so many ways, and who have given so much in return.

Life is all too brief and humans are transient. Similarly, water levels rise

Though the focus of this book is naturally the Cognashene area, the characteristics of its topography are shared with many parts of the Bay, and the unique quality of life in Cognashene cannot be solely attrib-uted to its basic elements.

As in most special places in the world, it is the people—the abo-riginals, the voyageurs, the explorers, the campers, the early settlers, the lumbermen, geologists, surveyors, engineers, artists, hoteliers, cot-tagers and year-round citizens—who have ultimately shaped the char-acter of Cognashene. Their roles and their contributions are cele-brated in this book. So, too, is the fact that there still remain within the boundaries of Cognashene places where the presence of man is

and fall, the fish population surges and ebbs, the winds come and go, even the pines flourish and wither. Only the granite remains unchanged, solid and enduring, a compelling link between the peo-ple and times gone by and those yet to come.

For those of you who know and love Cognashene, this book offers beautiful and moving refinements of the obvious, and perhaps preach-es to the fully converted. For those of you who know Cognashene slightly or not at all, these pages can stand as a revelation of a very special place in the world, an act of homage to its people, past, pre-sent and future.

— DONALD MCGIBBON

IN THE BEGINNING

NATIVE ROOTS

COGNASHENE'S
FIRST PEOPLE

Life Among the Huron

LONG AFTER THE LAST GLACIER DEPARTED THE BAY, BUT still centuries before the early cottagers descended, the first people to live around the southeast end of Georgian Bay had a unique impression of the world. Without benefit of maps or charts or anything even approaching a modern perspective they imagined themselves living atop a large turtle's shell, surrounded by oceans. And curiously, they understood that theirs was but a small corner of this vast Turtle Island.

Such was the prevalent theory at the turn of the seventeenth century, when the scenic stretch of land that lay between Lake Simcoe and the southeastern corner of Georgian Bay was the territory of the Huron confederacy and the most densely settled area of aboriginal Canada. Cognashene (though as yet unnamed), with its clusters of craggy islands, was part of this area. In fact, the Huron's own name for themselves was Ouendat (pronounced "Wendat"), an aboriginal term meaning "Islanders" or "Dwellers on a Peninsula." It wasn't until the French arrived and likened the native's cropped hair to the bristles on the neck of a wild boar ("*hure,*" in French) that the name Huron came about.

The Ouendat were primarily an agrarian people who found the fertile south end of the Bay well suited to the cultivation of corn, squash and

beans. To augment their crops, they also fished, hunted and gathered wild fruit, much of which they dried and stored for the winter. They lived in wooden longhouses in palisaded villages and attempted to live a quiet existence. Peace, however, would elude the Huron.

Shortly after the turn of the century the first Europeans began arriving at the Great Lakes, eager to trade their manufactured goods for furs and to initiate their mission work among the natives. They found the Huron—sometimes called "the good Iroquois"—allied to the Algonquian bands of the Canadian shield and the Petun tribe of the Collingwood area. Together, this trio controlled access to the lands north of the Great Lakes and the abundant natural resources of the Canadian Shield, resources their rivals and relatives to the south, the Iroquois of what is today northern New York state, were determined to access. If it was trade the French wanted they were obliged to align themselves with the Huron. The Iroquois had formed their own trading ties to the British and Dutch.

The first European to reach Georgian Bay was undoubtedly Etienne Brûlé, a clever but illiterate young Frenchman sent by Samuel de Champlain, explorer and governor of New France, to live among the Huron. The year was 1610 and the eighteen-year-old's mission was to study his hosts' language and customs, to scout the territory and presumably to foster goodwill and friendly trade. In exchange, Champlain invited Savignon, a Huron youth, to travel with him to France.

Savignon's adventure lasted but a year. He returned to his people full of stories of the savage French lifestyle and of streets full of beggars. Brûlé, in contrast, had adapted beautifully. It wasn't long before he spoke the language fluently and adopted the native style of dress, and the Huron, who were just as pleased with their young visitor as he was with them, invited him to stay indefinitely. Alas, Brûlé,

JOHN DAVID KELLY EXERCISED HIS
ARTISTIC LICENCE IN 1895 WHEN
HE PAINTED CHAMPLAIN'S 1615
ARRIVAL AT GEORGIAN BAY; NOTE
THE HEIGHT OF ROCK IN THE
DISTANCE. BRESSANI CREATED
THIS IMAGINATIVE MAP (OPPOSITE)
IN 1657 AND ILLUSTRATED IT WITH
DEPICTIONS OF INDIAN LIFE.

The Legend of Giant's Tomb Island

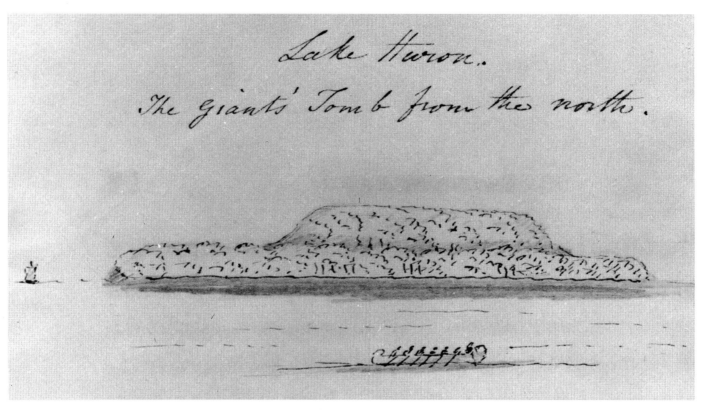

Lake Huron.

The Giants' Tomb from the north.

DR. J. J. BIGSBY OF THE BOUNDARY COMMISSION CREATED THIS SKETCH OF GIANT'S TOMB IN 1823.

KITCHIKEWANA IS AN IMMENSE figure in native history. A Huron god and protector who lived on the shores of Georgian Bay, he was also a giant with a larger-than-life temper to match. Romantically rebuffed by the beautiful Wanakita, who had already met the warrior of her dreams, the heartbroken Kitchikewana—always a little high-strung at the best of times—flew into a rage. Standing on Beausoleil Island, he scooped up huge clumps of earth and granite and began flinging them against the opposite shore, dozens, even hundreds, at a time. When he was done, an exhausted Kitchikewana took two steps from the island and lay down to sleep, his body forming the ghostly Giant's Tomb silhouette.

Some say that the earth and rock he flung that day landed in the water, forming the Thirty Thousand Islands, now a popular and picturesque cottage area. The splashes he created landed farther inland where a system of small lakes came to be, and the series of deep bays that run along the south shore are the result, they say, of Kitchikewana's hands gouging out the handfuls of earth.

Today Giant's Tomb Island is part of the Awenda Provincial Park, a favourite destination for picnickers, snorkelers, swimmers and campers.

who was unable to write, left no record of his life among the Indians.

When Champlain first visited the area in 1615 it was largely to assuage the Huron, whose interest in trading furs was marginal at best. Ever nervous about their Iroquois neighbours, and cognizant of the vulnerability of their trade route to New France, the Huron were far more intrigued by the prospect of securing French reinforcements in the event of an attack.

In order for their furs to reach the voracious European market, the Huron paddled them up the eastern shore of the Bay to the mouth of the French River, then followed the river to Lake Nipissing, along a series of portages to Trout Lake, the Mattawa River, the Ottawa River and eventually to their destination at Quebec. The length, difficulty and exposure of this voyage left the Huron wide-open to attack, a fact of which they were painfully aware.

Help us out against our enemy, they seemed to say, and *then* we'll talk furs.

During his own voyage, Champlain, who travelled south by canoe through the Thirty Thousand Islands and Cognashene, declared the Bay "*La Mère Douce*" (The Freshwater Sea) in the first written record of the area. The wild beauty of the Bay's rocky, pine-clad islands seemed lost on the explorer who described, with some relief, his first impressions of Huronia's rolling green landscape:

> *Here we found a great change in the country, this part being very fine, mostly cleared, with many hills and several streams, which make it an agreeable district. It seemed to me very pleasant in contrast to such a bad country as that through which we had come.*[2]

THE HURON HAD MUCH TO CONTEND WITH DURING THE FIRST half of the seventeenth century. Though the Iroquois were their most persistent adversaries, the French missionaries—those who were so determined to save the souls of the Godless natives— wreaked their own havoc on the nation. At the very least, it is certain they brought more than just religion to the region. Smallpox and other deadly diseases, against which the Indians had no natural immunity, arrived in Huronia at the same time

THE HURON GRINDING STONE (LEFT) AND GAMING STONES (BELOW) APPEAR RUSTIC IN CONTRAST TO THE COLOURED GLASS, FRENCH TRADING BEAD (ABOVE).

When Champlain first visited the area in 1615 it was largely to assuage the Huron, whose interest in trading furs was marginal at best.

as the French, and they ultimately ravaged Huronia. By 1639 the natives' once strong numbers had diminished dramatically from 25,000 to 9,000.

It was in this weakened state that Huronia continued to fight off its enemies until a final, decisive war with two nations of the Iroquois confederacy, the Mohawks and the Senecas, in March of 1649. This time, as the Iroquois pressed northwards from Lake Simcoe, the Huron fled their villages for the protection of Sainte Marie, a fortified Jesuit centre. En route, they received word that two Jesuits—Fathers Jean de Brébeuf and Gabriel Lalemant—had been tortured and burned at the stake. With the Iroquois hard on their heels the French set fire to their own sanctuary and fled with their followers to Christian Island (then known as Gahoendoe), where, without shelter or food supplies, they passed a devastating winter.[3]

Starvation and exposure became their greatest threats during this time: an estimated 5,000 died in the harsh winter of 1650.[4] In the spring, the survivors dispersed to neighbouring tribes—mainly to the south and west—shed the name Huron and officially adopted that of Wyandot (a variation on their original name, Ouendat). About 600 Huron, those who remained in league with the French, retained their name and followed the Jesuits east to the safety of their ancestral lands along the north shore of the St. Lawrence River.

A SKETCH BY C.W. JEFFERYS ILLUSTRATES THE TORTURE OF JESUIT FATHERS LALEMANT AND BREBEUF.

Encounters with Another First Nation

AFTER THE DESTRUCTION OF HURONIA, IT WAS MORE THAN A century before Europeans returned to Georgian Bay, and when they did they encountered the people of another first nation, the Ojibwa. By the 1700s this nation was the dominant force in a large area covering the northern shores of Lake Huron and Lake Superior and extending westward to the headwaters of the Mississippi and eastward to the St. Lawrence. It was the Ojibwa (an Algonquian nation) who named the rocky island community on the Bay's southeastern shore "Cognashene"—"the place of porcupines and blueberries."[5]

The Ojibwa lifestyle was very different from that of the Ouendat. They lived in widely dispersed communities of small mobile bands, each with its own chief to manage its own affairs. They erected dome-shaped wigwams in campsites close to their hunting and fishing grounds and handy for gathering wild rice and berries to store for the lean winter months. Present-day cottages in Cognashene may well be constructed where an Ojibwa base camp once existed.

During the latter half of the seventeenth century the canoe route from Georgian Bay to Montreal once again became a hotly contested war zone. This time it was the Ojibwa and Iroquois who clashed, with some of the fiercest battles taking place north of Cognashene in the Thirty Thousand Islands.

Closer to Cognashene a bigger and more decisive encounter occurred: the Battle of the Blue Mountains. Oral history indicates it was fought around 1700 near Penetanguishene, after the Ottawa and Ojibwa learned that a Mohawk war party of the dreaded Iroquois confederacy was advancing overland from Lake Simcoe. All available warriors, summoned to meet at Blue Mountain, moved down the Bay in a giant flotilla of 700 canoes to confront the aggressors.

Today, it is difficult to imagine such a massive military struggle on the tranquil shores of Georgian Bay, but a battle royal it was. This time the Ojibwa scored a decisive victory—and with relatively little bloodshed, thanks to the Ojibwa chief, Sahgimah, who persuaded his warriors to spare

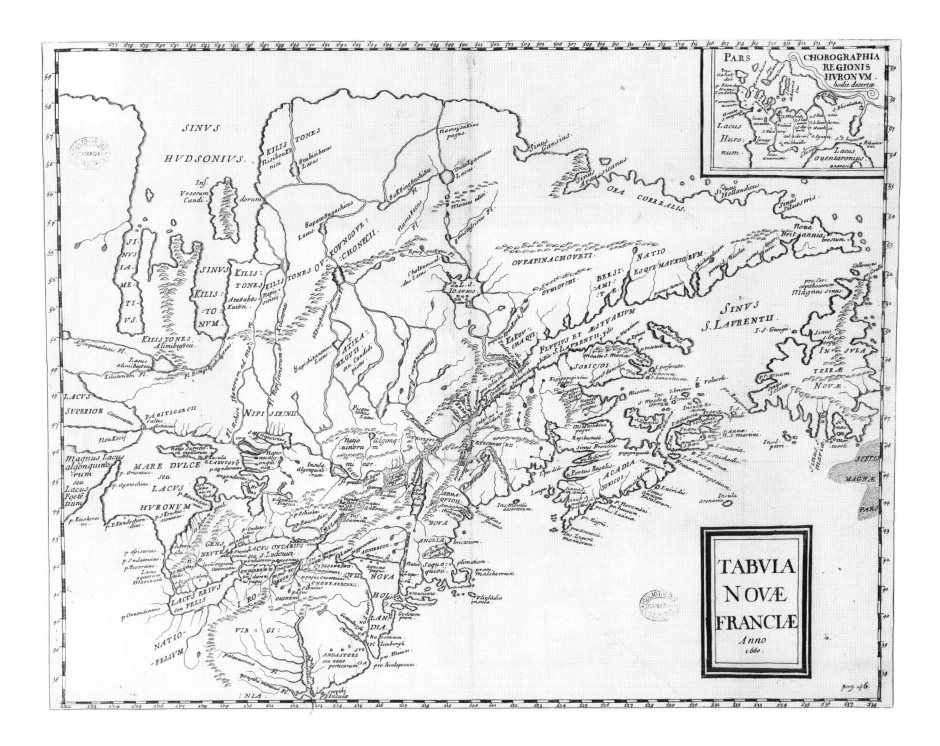

A DETAILED, THOUGH OBVIOUSLY INACCURATE, MAP OF GEORGIAN BAY AND LAKE ONTARIO, DRAWN BY DE CREUX IN 1660.

THE INSET IN THE TOP RIGHT-HAND CORNER REPRESENTS DE CREUX'S IMPRESSION OF THE NOW-DESERTED HURON REGION.

the lives of the defeated Mohawk. He was not without his reasons. "No, by the power of the Great Serpent we shall not slay these craven Mohawks," said the wise old chief; "we shall use them as messengers to go home to bring the news of what a Mohawk defeat means on the shore of our lake of the Ottawas."[6]

The First Wave of Newcomers

BY THE EARLY 1800S THE FRONTIER of European settlement was rapidly expanding northward where it encountered the Ojibwa in a weakened condition. Though they had fought on the British side against the Kitchi Mokoman, or American Long Knives, in the American Revolution, and again most valiantly in the War of 1812, the natives received scant reward for their loyal support. In the years following the war, though their population remained steady at 8,000, their impact as a military and political presence diminished.[7] Gradually, in a desperate attempt to survive, they began "surrendering" their hunting lands in southern Ontario, yielding the best of it to the steady tide of eager British and Loyalist settlers, while they withdrew to reserves on the margins.

Typical of the the government's callous conduct during these years was the debacle at Coldwater, where Sir John Colborne established an experimental reserve in 1830. His objective was to teach the impoverished Ojibwa the value of sedentary farming. Many of the 500 who moved to the reserve made a valiant attempt at working the fertile land, much like the Huron had before them. They managed to raise potatoes, corn, wheat and peas. But despite their best efforts they were hampered by a number of

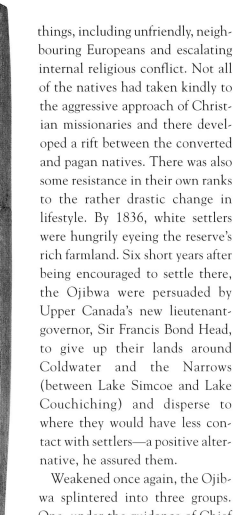

VARIOUS TOOLS, WEAPONS AND HOUSEHOLD ITEMS (OPPOSITE AND ABOVE) LEND CLUES TO THE HURON LIFESTYLE.

things, including unfriendly, neighbouring Europeans and escalating internal religious conflict. Not all of the natives had taken kindly to the aggressive approach of Christian missionaries and there developed a rift between the converted and pagan natives. There was also some resistance in their own ranks to the rather drastic change in lifestyle. By 1836, white settlers were hungrily eyeing the reserve's rich farmland. Six short years after being encouraged to settle there, the Ojibwa were persuaded by Upper Canada's new lieutenant-governor, Sir Francis Bond Head, to give up their lands around Coldwater and the Narrows (between Lake Simcoe and Lake Couchiching) and disperse to where they would have less contact with settlers—a positive alternative, he assured them.

Weakened once again, the Ojibwa splintered into three groups. One, under the guidance of Chief Snake, retreated to Snake Island in Lake Simcoe. Chief Yellowhead led his followers to Rama, near Lake Couchiching. And the largest party, led by Chief John Thomas Assance, settled on Georgian Bay's Beausoleil Island.

Clashing Over Land

THE OJIBWA SETTLEMENT ON BEAUSOLEIL was ill-fated from the start and lasted just twenty very difficult years. The Ojibwa were now farmers and found the conditions on the island untenable. The soil was sandy and lacking in nutrients. The only crop that grew was potatoes. Though the Ojibwa cleared 300 acres for farming, they still had to rely on fishing, hunting, berry picking and, worst of all, government assistance for their sustenance. This was a difficult time for the aboriginal settlers.

There was, however, one area of untapped revenue that the Ojibwa now eagerly pursued—that of developing business relations with the white settlers on the mainland, a large and receptive market for the abundant fish and timber from the islands. The pine logs cut by the natives were also vital to the construction of their own homes as they had long since eschewed wigwams in favour of log houses. It was only natural, then, that the natives complained in 1854 when they discovered a timber merchant blithely helping himself to trees on Christian Island. This was not part of the land they had ceded. By the time the Indian commissioner, Captain Thomas G. Anderson, responded to their complaint, much of the best timber had already been removed.

This event coincided with the Ojibwa Council's campaign to move the Beausoleil Island community to better farmland somewhere along the south shore of Georgian Bay. Though it sounded reasonable, their request was futile, given the government's policy to keep the natives segregated.

SIR FRANCIS BOND HEAD, 1873.

Eventually, however, a compromise was suggested. The Ojibwa could have their new island, but only by surrendering Beausoleil and most of their other islands.

In 1856, the Chiefs and Principal Men of the Chippewa Indians (the name now used for this branch of the Ojibwa people) from Lake Simcoe and Lake Couchiching, as well as from Beausoleil, signed Treaty No. 76 with representatives of Queen Victoria. Under this treaty the natives surrendered to the Crown four islands in Lake Simcoe, one in Lake Couchiching and "all those islands lying and being in the Georgian Bay, Lake Huron, heretofore claimed by our tribe" save "that group of islands known as the Christian Islands."

In return the Chippewa would receive all of the revenue from the sale of the islands, a portion of which was to be used to build a church on Christian Island. The remainder would be invested with the interest to be paid annually "to us, our people and children, in all time coming."

The three Christian Islands reserved for the natives comprise what we refer to today as Beckwith, Hope and, by far the largest, Christian Island. It was to the latter that most of the Beausoleil Island natives moved. By the end of the 1860s, Cognashene was left wide open to timber companies and future bands of summer settlers.

But the 1856 surrender of islands was not the only treaty with Indians

The Robinson Treaties, 1850

THERE HAVE BEEN MANY DISPUTES about the Robinson treaties, some of which are still not settled. One of particular concern to Cognashene pertains to the Thirty Thousand Islands. Though the written text of the Huron Treaty specifically refers to "the Islands" opposite the eastern and northern shores of Lake Huron, from Penetanguishene to Sault Ste. Marie, the Georgian Bay Ojibwa have a different understanding of what was actually said in the treaty council. They maintain that Robinson only asked them to cede "aki," the anishinabe word for land or soil, not "minis," their word for islands.[11]

Obviously, this is a major point of difference. In their view they never agreed to surrender the windswept islands which they valued as a refuge from mosquitoes and other biting insects in the late spring and summer, and as fishing stations in the fall.[12] The Crown's advisors however, stood by the written version of the treaties. Governments granted timber cutting rights on the islands and eventually began selling them off to summer cottagers.

No. 61.

Entered in Letter Surrender Book
Pages 139, 140, 141, 142
& 143

Surrender

By the Ojibewa Indians
Inhabiting the North Shore of
Lake Huron

Recorded in the Office of the
Provincial Registrar, this 22d day of
November — in Lib. "C. M. Miscellaneous
Folio 1. &c

The Ojibwa chiefs were well aware of the British law and began to pressure colonial authorities to stop the encroachments on their land.

relating to Georgian Bay. In September, 1850, the Robinson-Huron and Robinson-Superior Treaties were signed between agents of the Crown and representatives of the Ojibwa Nation of northern Lakes Huron and Superior. Named for William Benjamin Robinson, a member of the provincial legislature and younger brother of Chief Justice John Beverley Robinson, who negotiated them on behalf of the government, these treaties addressed a vast area of northern Ontario, all of the north shore of Lake Superior, and the north and east shores of Lake Huron, including the east shore of Georgian Bay.

The Robinson treaties were triggered by the encroachment of the resource industries in the upper Great Lakes. By the 1840s, Americans were buying timber cut by white squatters near Sault Ste. Marie and along the north shore of Lake Huron. The government of the United Colony of Canada was licensing prospectors to explore for minerals—mainly copper—and encouraging companies to start up mines in the same area.

All of this development was taking place on Ojibwa lands and in violation of the Proclamation of 1763, a document issued by King George III outlining imperial policies in relation to the native lands. It stipulated that only the Crown could purchase lands in native territory and made illegal the acquisition of lands through unscrupulous methods. This Proclamation remains part of Canadian law to this day.[8]

The Ojibwa chiefs were well aware of the British policy and began to pressure the colonial authorities to stop the encroachments on their lands until a proper treaty had been made. Matters came to a head in the fall of 1849. By then, mining companies had begun operating in unceded areas. In reaction, the Ojibwa seized the property of the Quebec and Lake Superior Mining Company to force government intervention and focus attention on the government's neglect of its responsibilities. This was known as the Mica Bay Uprising.

As insurrections go, it was relatively tame. The idea was to hold and operate the mine under native supervision until their claims were recognized. By the time news of it reached Toronto, however, it was portrayed in the media as a full-scale native uprising. The government promptly dispatched 100 of Toronto's finest from its Rifle Brigade overland to Nottawasaga Bay. If residents of Cognashene had been looking west on the morning of Novem-

A COMPASS, SEXTANT
AND FLINT-LOCK MUSKET:
SURE SIGNS THAT THE
EUROPEANS HAD ARRIVED.

TWO OJIBWA WOMEN FROM CHRISTIAN ISLAND ARRIVE ON THE SHORES OF COGNASHENE IN THE THIRTIES, BRINGING WITH THEM THE QUILL BOXES, MINIATURE CANOES AND BEADED MOCCASINS THEY HOPED TO SELL. ON THE RETURN TRIP, THEY WOULD CARRY THE BLUEBERRIES THEY PICKED DURING THEIR VISIT.

ber 19th, they might have spotted a puff of smoke from the steamer *Gore* as she charged up the Bay with the Toronto Rifles aboard. The *Gore* never made it to Mica Bay. She became locked in the ice near the Sault where the soldiers spent a chilly winter barricaded in a Hudson's Bay trading post.[9]

Shingwakonce (an Ojibwa chief) and several other "instigators" were subsequently charged with criminal offences, but the charges were quickly thrown out by Chief Justice Robinson.[10] Still, the uprising did quicken the colonial government's interest in negotiating a treaty with the Ojibwa. In January 1850, William Robinson was appointed treaty commissioner, and by April he was up at the Sault preparing for negotiations. The actual signing of the treaties—one with the Ojibwa of Lake Superior, the other with the Ojibwa of Lake Huron and Georgian Bay—was a solemn event mixing British and Ojibwa ceremonial custom.

The main proceedings took place around a traditional Council Fire in a Hudson Bay warehouse with colourful Red Coat soldiers and Ojibwa warriors standing in the background. No official records of the event survive, but historians speculate that the meetings opened and closed with the smoking of the traditional opwagan, or ceremonial pipe. There were long speeches by Robinson and

A HANDSOME COLLECTION OF CHRISTIAN ISLAND QUILL BOXES.

many of the Ojibwa chiefs and Principal Men. One of the interpreters was John William Keating, whose father had been garrison adjutant at Penetanguishene and whose family name is now borne by one of Cognashene's islands and channels.

In return for ceding a vast territory, the natives received some small reserves, a cash payment and an annuity. Seventeen reserves were selected by the Ojibwa and a total cash payment of just over £2,000 was arranged. It's estimated that this amounted to about $20 per family—in those days, a third or half the annual wage of an unskilled labourer. The annuity was set at £600, or about $6 per family, though the treaties hint-

ed that if the ceded lands yielded sufficient revenue, the annual payment would be increased by £1 per person or a greater sum that "Her Majesty may be graciously pleased to order." This never came to pass.

IN THE 1890S THE FEDERAL AND PROVINCIAL GOVERNMENTS agreed to draw a demarcation line at Moose Deer Point. North of it, the Ontario government was given control of the islands, while the Canadian government would administer the islands to the south. The proceeds from timber licences and the sale of islands south of Moose Deer Point—which would presumably include the islands of Cognashene—were to be put in trust by the government for "the benefit of the Chippewas of Lakes Huron and Simcoe."

Today, the descendants of those Chippewa form the Beausoleil First Nation, a community of more than 1,000 people centred on Christian Island. Like other first nations, it is in the process of reasserting its right to self-government. The community's elected council administers a wide range of services—including an elementary school, a network of roads, a police force, youth and elders' programs and a ferry service to the mainland. Even on frosty winter days, the good ship *Indian Maiden* cuts through several inches of ice, conveying commuters, schoolchildren and visitors across the two miles of "open" between Christian Island and Cedar Point. A principal source of income for the community is construction, much of it on the 180 sites that are leased to summer cottagers.

Only a handful of elders on Christian Island can still recall the trips they used to make to the Cognashene area when they would fill their rowboats with sweet-grass and porcupine quill baskets, beaded moccasins and miniature birch-bark canoes to sell at cottage docks and to steamboat passengers. On the return trip, their cargo would consist of baskets of blueberries and hampers of gulls' eggs garnered from the outer islands. Often, rough waters would force them to take shelter for a day or two on Giant's Tomb or Beckwith Island before they could carry on for home.

Sadly, the Ojibwa stopped coming to Cognashene altogether about thirty years ago, around the same time most of the islands became occupied.

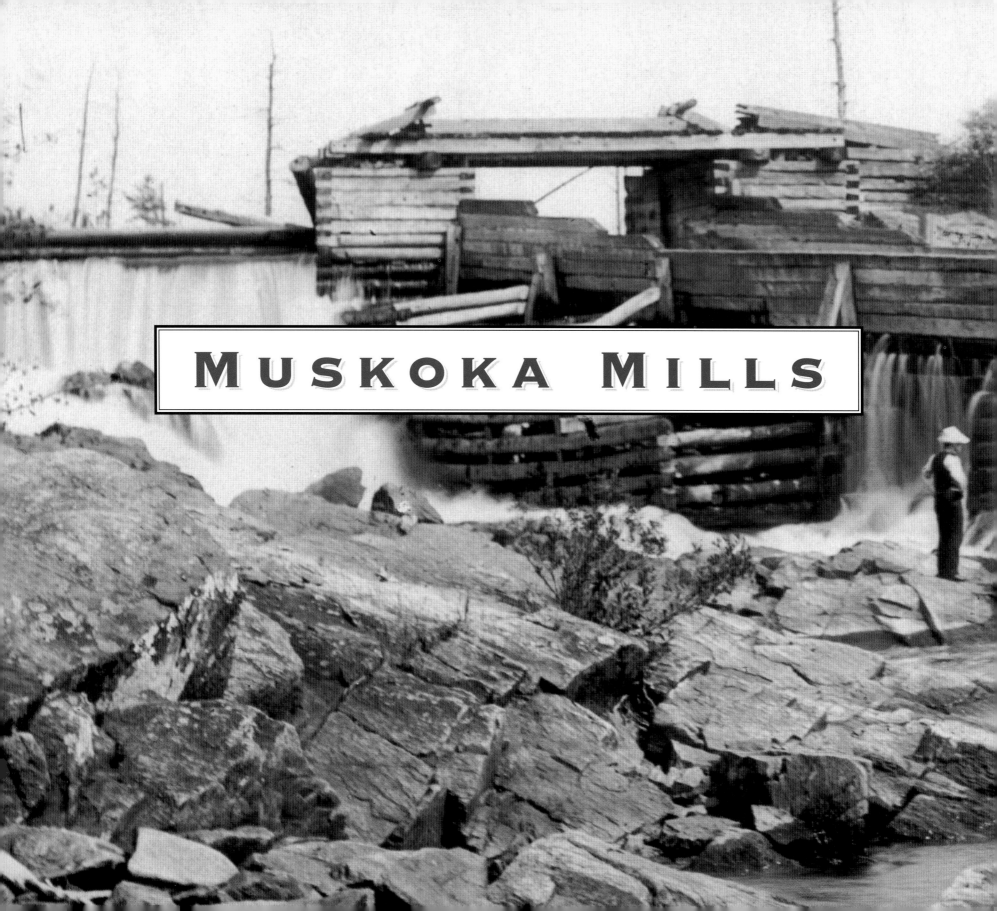

Muskoka Mills

LUMBERING
IN COGNASHENE

In the dark, tangled forest where lumberjacks sing,
And their saws and their axes, the music will ring
Oh the nights they are weary and the days they are long,
But my comrades they cheer me with music and song.
— The Maid From Tidehead

The Lumber Frontier

THE STORY OF THE LUMBER BOOM IN CANADA IS THE STORY of the country's early industry, of eager entrepreneurs and the hardy woodsmen they employed. It is also the history of one of Canada's primary trades during its years of development, a trade that was, for a time, the backbone of the nation's economy.[1]

Canada's lumber business first blossomed near the beginning of the nineteenth century, and it boomed for the next hundred years, expanding westward with the developing country. As the early demand from Britain, Canada's first big customer, exhausted the supply of timber from the great pine forests of New Brunswick, Quebec and the Ottawa Valley, the industry looked to the woods around the Trent and Muskoka river systems.

After a time, the Canadian market was also driven by America's insatiable appetite for lumber, particularly after 1835, when U.S. settlement pushed westward and outgrew its own supply of timber along the way. This demand was relatively easy to satisfy. The American market had less discriminating "timber taste" than the British. Planks and boards of virtually any quality were acceptable—a far cry from the top-grade, square-cut timber demanded by the United Kingdom.[2]

But it wasn't only the demand for wood placing pressure on Canada's forests. As the young country expanded west and north, settlers in search of prime agricultural land ultimately clashed with the wilderness. In the mid-nineteenth century, many came to the area around Georgian Bay with an eye to farming, and the tall, thick stands of pine merely stood in their way. Today we mourn the loss of the forests from our shores, but in those days the notion of preserving woodlands for future generations may not have occurred to early conservationists.

Besides, the wood was being put to good use and the mills employed many men, whose long days in the lumber camps were ordered by grinding routine. Songs and stories, poker games, drinking and Saturday evening square dances entertained the men during their few hours off.[3]

Ironically, it was this very life of monotony that spawned the kinds of traditions and legends that make such fascinating folklore today. Some even say it inspired a lingo all its own. ("Skid road," "jobber," and "in a jam" are just some of the many logging-related expressions born of this time.) But more than that, it produced a breed of skilled, hard-working men who were as ready as they were rough, a colourful bunch of pioneers who plied their tough trade in a harsh and unforgiving landscape.[4]

Such men played a supporting role in the logging of Cognashene. Their bosses, the mill owners, were the leading men.

Mapping a Path for Logging

IN ORDER TO BE SUCCESSFUL, A LUMBER OPERATION REQUIRED two things: an almost endless supply of timber and a river big enough and fast enough to carry the logs from their source to open water. Once there, they could be transferred to the railway or onto ships for the remainder of the journey. In both respects, Cognashene was ripe for the picking.

There are many early maps of Georgian Bay and the region lying between it and the Ottawa River, but the interior region with its intricate river systems remained undefined for many years. War with the United

(THIS PAGE) BOATERS EXPLORE AN ENORMOUS LOG BOOM CORRALLED IN A MILLPOND BY A RING OF LOGS WHICH ARE CHAINED END TO END. (PREVIOUS PAGE) A RARE GLIMPSE OF A MUSKOKA MILLS LOG SLIDE IN THE 1890S.

HENRY BAYFIELD'S 1822
CHART OF GEORGIAN BAY
(SHOWN HERE, ALONG WITH
HIS INSTRUMENTS) WAS
THE FIRST TO DEFINE THE
ISLANDS OF COGNASHENE.

LAY OF THE LAND: THE VILLAGE OF MUSKOKA MILLS AS SEEN FROM LONGUISSA POINT, ACROSS THE BAY.

States in 1812, and the importance of the fur trade in the developing economy, demanded accurate information on the various water routes. In 1818, Henry W. Bayfield of the Royal Navy began charting Lake Huron, which included Georgian Bay, as part of the Great Lakes Survey. The resulting charts, which were produced in 1822, were the first to include the region known as Cognashene, and the first to name Georgian Bay in honour of the reigning monarch, King George IV.

IN MARCH 1837 A FURTHER SURVEY OF THE AREA BETWEEN THE Ottawa River and Lake Huron was ordered in the hope of establishing a practical water route. Three parties were formed, one to explore the French River/Lake Nipissing route, a second to investigate the Magnetawan, and a third, under the direction of sixty-seven-year-old David Thompson, to map the Muskoka system.

Thompson, who had made a name for himself charting the Columbia River, set out with his survey party by canoe in July 1837, and headed up the Musquash River to make "the first detailed survey of the lakes and rivers of the Muskoka chain."[5]

Mill Operations on the Musquash

THE FIRST REPORT OF A SAWMILL ON THE MUSQUASH RIVER was made by Alexander Murray who, unaware of Thompson's detailed survey, set out to chart the very same area sixteen years later, in the spring of 1853. After completing his survey, Murray submitted his report to the provincial geological authorities in February 1854. In it he observed that, "Since the time of my visit, Mr. W.B. Hamilton, of Penetanguishene, has erected a sawmill on or near the first falls, about two miles from the mouth of the river, where he is said to have an almost inexhaustible supply of pine within easy distance. Should this attempt at lumbering prove successful, and the present prices for the manufactured article continue, it is not improbable that establishments may extend still further into the interior before many years, as the river affords every facility for using water power in a great many places."[6]

William Hamilton was an early entrepreneur from Penetanguishene. While still a successful fur trader there, he purchased timber rights on the

THE NEW FOUR-STOREY MILL, COMPLETED IN 1879, FEATURED A WATER-LEVEL ENTRANCEWAY (ON THE LEFT), A SAWDUST CARRIER (CLIMBING UPHILL TO THE RIGHT), AND AN IMPRESSIVE PROCESSING CAPACITY OF 100,000 BOARD FEET EVERY TWENTY-FOUR HOURS.

Musquash River in 1853, erected a mill at its mouth and concentrated his sales in the booming Chicago market. His mill was located above what later became known as the Shingle Mill Dam in the heart of a huge tract of pine—the future home of Muskoka Mills.

Hamilton's timing couldn't have been worse. A drastic decline in the lumber market forced him to sell the business in 1857 to Charles Kelly of Collingwood, and other speculators from Chicago and Buffalo, for $16,000. Unfortunately, the new partnership was no more successful; despite Hamilton's advice to proceed cautiously, the business failed with the new owners still owing Hamilton most of the purchase price.

Hamilton, while unsuccessful as a big businessman, was nevertheless instrumental in Collingwood's development. He laid out the town, had the area surveyed and engineered much of its early growth. For his efforts he was eventually appointed mayor.

The Muskoka Mill & Lumber Co.

HAMILTON AND KELLY WEREN'T THE ONLY ENTREPRENEURS TO try their hands at logging. After Kelly went out of business, J. Tyson of Collingwood stepped up to the plate. For most of the 1860s he struggled to maintain the mill on the Musquash, but with little success. In 1861 the mill lay idle, and though demand from America was to grow steadily over the next decade, Tyson withdrew from the business in 1869, selling it to Lewis Hotchkiss and J. C. Hughson, two American lumbermen intent on making inroads into the Canadian market. With the greatest sources of American lumber—the forests of Pennsylvania and Michigan—rapidly thinning out after the mid-1860s, these experienced timber merchants (and others like them) not only looked north of the border for fresh supply, they began to establish their own operations in Canada.

During the mid- to late-nineteenth century the shores of Georgian Bay were dotted with lumber mills and timber rights: Port Severn, Parry Sound, Waubaushene, Collingwood, Muskoka Mills. By the early 1870s, many of the Bay's mills had passed through several hands, eventually to be bought, either partially (as was the case with Muskoka Mills) or outright, by the ambitious young Anson Phelps Dodge. As head of the newly formed Georgian Bay Lumber Company, Dodge seemed well on his way to realizing his dream of a lumber empire on the shores of the Bay.

Like many of the early Ontario mill owners, A.G.P. Dodge, as he was known, was American, the son of the wealthy and wise William Earl Dodge of New York. Young Anson came by his interest in the lumber industry honestly. His father's company, Phelps Dodge, owned large lumbering operations in Pennsylvania and some of the southern states and had strong international ties. However, if he inherited his father's inclination, Anson failed to observe his sound business practices. Ignoring the volatility of the lumber trade, he paid a premium for the mills in the Muskoka, Parry Sound and Byng Inlet areas, and quickly built or renovated "no fewer than eight sawmills."[7] And like poor Hamilton before him, his timing couldn't have been worse. A business recession soon forced lumber prices down—and Dodge Jr. into bankruptcy.

With his son drowning in financial hot water—forced to sell his assets at fire-sale prices—Dodge Sr. came to the rescue. As his father set about unravelling the mess he'd made, Dodge Jr. disappeared from Canada for good. Ironically, the disgraced Anson's fortunes would dwindle even further; the one-time millionaire who had been determined to dominate the lumber industry, and had even dabbled a little in Canadian politics, eventually exhausted his inheritance. He lived out his life in a small Chicago hotel, and when he died in May 1918, he left just $50,000 to his daughter.[8]

The troubled operation at Muskoka Mills (which was still going by the name of J.C. Hughson & Co. at the time) was salvaged by Dodge Sr. who formed a consortium of seven businessmen, most of them experienced lumbermen. In January 1875, William Dodge and his cohorts (Titus B. Meigs of New Jersey, J.C. Hughson and N.H. Salisbury of New York, J.S. Huntoon of Collins Bay, Theodore W. Buck of Waubaushene, and Archibald Hamilton Campbell Sr. of Toronto) signed the original charter of the Muskoka Mill & Lumber Company. Campbell became its first president.

The new company fell heir to five existing mills at the mouth of the Musquash, a sawmill, a timber mill, two lath mills and a shingle mill, as well as docks and about twenty houses and buildings. In addition, there were eleven tugs, scows and barges, two or three of which now rest on the bottom of the Musquash River or in some of the adjoining bays.

An early directors' meeting held in Albany in August 1875, determined that first and foremost a new sawmill was in order. Plans were also made to take out ten million board feet of pine in the coming winter. It's not clear whether this ambitious program was ever undertaken, because a year later in August 1876, in an abrupt about-face, the directors decided not to harvest any stock during the winter, or to proceed with the erection of the new mill. The superintendent's contract wasn't renewed and the president's salary was to cease in February 1877, if there was no work being done. The once-booming timber industry was in the midst of yet another depression.

WHILE THE LUMBER MARKET WASN'T TO RECOVER FULLY for a decade, things began to look better by the next year. In August 1877, it was estimated that there were three million feet of timber in the millpond. If this sold, the directors optimistically specified that another eight to ten million feet could be taken out in the winter. They also approved the construction of "a stop log dam" in the river at Muskosch Shute, later known as Shingle Mill Dam.[9] The base of this can still be seen under the rushing water at the Shingle Mill rapids. It seems the intention was to raise an already existing dam another five feet and to enlarge the millpond. The dam also forced open the eastern most channel of the river, which flowed over sixteen-foot falls and emptied into the Bay about three-quarters of a mile to the east of the present mouth of the river.

Photographs from this time are rare, but it appears that the water ran right through the village and was used to power the mill machinery. The crib works in the millpond, which are still in evidence today, were designed to secure log booms. These holding booms were used to contain logs until they were needed at the various mills.

These were years of flux for the Muskoka Mill operators. Key players would come and go, expansions and acquisitions were authorized and then, at the last minute, cancelled. In August 1878, Dodge and Meigs withdrew from the company, followed shortly after by Buck. Now Campbell and Hughson controlled the operations. The number of directors was reduced to three—Campbell, Hughson and Huntoon—who agreed to build

A MUSKOKA MILLS COMPANY LEDGER FROM 1888; A SAW BLADE AND AXE FROM THE SAME ERA.

MONTH OF *August*

TIME BOOK FOR THE

OCCUPATION.	1	2	3	4	5	6	7	8	9	10	11	12	13	14	15	16	17	18	19	20	21	22	23	24	25	26	27	28	29	30	31	Total Time.	Rate.	Amount

NAME.

Wm. Carmichael

All in a Day's Work

THE SHIPS THAT PLIED THE waters of Georgian Bay in the service of the mills made their marks in more ways than one. As a result of fluctuating water levels and a dearth of reliable charting information in the last century, several left their names on shoals, others sunk from sight altogether.

Just east of Longuissa Point is WALES ROCK, discovered no doubt by some unfortunate skipper of the 238-ton steam tug, the *Wales*. Built in 1864 at Brockville and owned by Chaffy Bros., then by Hotchkiss, and later by Hughson & Co., she rests today near the entrance to Longuissa Bay, having served as a houseboat in her final years.

East of Wales Rock is CLIFTON BAY, at least part of which is still filled with sawdust. It is also the rumoured resting place of the hull of the side-wheel steamer, the *Clifton*, built in 1855 and owned by Hotchkiss. After removing her machinery in 1867, Hotchkiss used the ship as a barge until retiring her, permanently, to the bottom of the bay.

Built in Quebec in 1867, the 125-foot-long schooner *Otonabee* was a lumber carrier of 225 tons. She was owned by A.H. Campbell & Co. and sold to the Muskoka Mill & Lumber Co. in 1881. In November 1880, after being loaded with lumber and shingles at Muskoka Mills and towed by a tug out to Giant's Tomb Island, she attempted to sail her way to Tobermory. A strong nor'wester ripped through her sails and blew her back to Collingwood. Just off the southeast shore of Arthurs' Island, in the Musquash Channel, lies the OTONABEE SHOAL, marked by a green buoy.

South of the Otonabee Shoal is the HOTCHKISS ROCK on the main channel from Honey Harbour to Cognashene, just outside the Muskoka Landing Channel. The rock is named for the tug, the *Freddy Hotchkiss*, which, piloted by A.H. Campbell Jr., ran aground on it while heading for (or from) Penetang in the mid-1880s. The tug's first name has also been perpetuated in the long, narrow FREDDY CHANNEL, which ran from the mills to Muskoka Landing.

The massive lumber barge, the *Lewis Hotchkiss*, was built in Collingwood in 1872. At 1001 tons, with a capacity of one million feet of lumber, she was estimated to have been the largest wooden ship built there at that time. At her launch she got stuck on the ways and had to be warped off, only to be wrecked in 1891, twenty-five miles west of Goderich, en route from Muskoka Mills.

The *Chippewa* was built in 1874 and registered to the Muskoka Mills. She weighed 132 tons, was ninety-four feet long and had a beam of almost twenty-four feet. Sarnia was her port of call. It is believed that her hull now rests on the bottom of the Musquash River where she attracts scuba divers during the summer months. Further up river, below the shingle mill rapids, lie the ribs and remains of the barge *Ontario*, which was sold by Hotchkiss to Hughson and Dodge in 1871.

---

a new frame for the lumber mill and move the mill to the mouth of the new river.

At a special general meeting of the shareholders held in September of that year, the idea of a mortgage first arose. The directors needed to borrow money in order to finance the new mill and to pay off certain liabilities still owing to William Dodge. The mortgage was approved and work at the mill proceeded.

A new four-storey building went up between 1878 and 1879, the capacity of which was impressive. Its circular and gang saws were able to process 100,000 board feet every twenty-four hours. (The term "board feet" indicates the common unit of measurement for both lumber and sawlogs: twelve inches wide, one inch thick, twelve inches long.) Scows and barges conveniently loaded the processed lumber straight from the mill's water-level, ground-floor opening.

Again in 1879, there were signs of trouble ahead. In May of that year an agreement with J.C. Hughson & Co. to purchase mill machinery in Sarnia was cancelled. Despite the fact that in August 1880, the directors approved a plan for "thirteen million feet to be taken out during the ensuing winter,"[10] the mills didn't operate during the winter months at all, though a caretaker was engaged to ensure the safety of the mill and works.

It's likely that most of the employees were up the river cutting the timber that was to be sent to the mills for processing the following spring.

By 1881 the company's board of directors had become a bi-family affair, consisting of two Hughsons and two Campbells (both father-son teams). In December 1884, Campbell Sr. purchased all of the shares held by the Hughsons. Not surprisingly, the following year the elected directors were Campbell and his three sons, J.H. Mayne Campbell, Colin G. Campbell and A.H. Campbell Jr.

In March 1887, yet another special general meeting of the shareholders approved the expansion of the company's purview to include driving, booming, towing and sorting of logs, the transport of lumber, grain, coal and all other goods including mail and passengers, plus the acquisition of offices and yards in Ontario for the sale or disposal of lumber and other building supplies and materials.

It appears that the mill operations continued for the next ten years and apparently with greater success, for the company was able to pay healthy dividends of forty-five per cent. But with the timber limits owned by the company approaching exhaustion, the sawmills at Muskoka Mills were eventually closed in 1895. This was a clear foreshadowing of what lay in store for the Bay's other, still successful, mills.

In January 1898, the shareholders discussed the dissolution of the company, and the directors were authorized to take the necessary steps. However, they didn't proceed and the company remained in existence for another hundred years. The charter was finally surrendered in 1991.

The Village of Muskoka Mills

SIGNS OF A VILLAGE AT MUSKOKA MILLS WERE REPORTED AS EARLY as 1853, around the time Hamilton made his ill-fated attempt at lumbering, but it wasn't until 1867 that any real record appeared. This was a company village built to house the employees, whose numbers swelled to 400 during the mill's heyday.

Life in the remote hamlet was quiet in the winter when most of the men were out in the bush cutting timber to feed the mills. This was the ideal time to harvest, when the rivers and inland lakes were frozen and sleighs could haul logs over the deep layers of snow. It isn't difficult to imagine that for many of the men, away from their families for extended periods of time, it was a cold and lonely existence. Their days were long, their nights were short, and Sunday was their only day off. And even then, most men devoted their day of "rest" to laundry and other camp-related chores.

The warmer weather—the time of the river drives, when the logs were propelled downstream—brought more activity to the village. Ships belonging to the mills ferried people from Muskoka Landing, a company-owned dock three miles away on Maxwell Island (later known as Whalen's), and steamboats ran from Penetanguishene and Midland to the landing almost daily during the navigation season.

By 1875 there were about twenty houses in the village, in addition to the five mills. Sometime after 1883, Archibald Hamilton Campbell Jr., who was to become manager of the mills, as well as Justice of the Peace

The Legend of Sandy Gray

O NE SUNDAY IN 1867, SANDY Gray tempted the fates, and for his courage he is at the centre of the most oft-repeated tale about logging in Cognashene. The larger-than-life foreman of the Musquash gang was probably always a little full of bluster and bravado. So when, on that particular day, a log jam on the river threatened to slow the company's production, it was no surprise that Gray was the first to act. "Boys," he exclaimed, "we'll break the jam or breakfast in hell"[10] (an apparent reference to the Sabbath). Gray managed both on that day. He freed the logs but the turbulent thrust of their breaking apart swiftly carried the lumberjack over a waterfall to his death.

Gray's body was retrieved about a mile below the falls, which still bear his name today. His men buried him in a shallow grave between two tall and stately pines close to the river's edge. His grave was marked by a board carved simply with the words, "Alex Gray, 1867."

Some of the houses burned in a legendary sawdust fire that smouldered underground for many years until it finally extinguished itself in 1910.

and postmaster in the village, had his own house on the shore to the east of the mills. For a time he lived there year round. In 1887, his father, Archibald Sr., built the family's splendid summer home, Longuissa, on a point directly across from the mills.

In the centre of the "county post office on the Muskoka River" were the four spillways, traces of which can still be seen.[11] From these waterfalls, which have a drop of approximately sixteen feet, the water power was harnessed to drive the mills with their circular saws, two large gang saws and a fine band saw.

The main dock extended 100 yards into the bay. Along the shoreline of Rennie's Bay extensive docks were built out twenty feet or so from the shore. These were the piling grounds in the form of large wooden cribs filled with rocks which can still be seen underwater. The freshly cut lumber was stacked along these shores to dry during the summer, and in the fall, natives from Christian Island were employed to help load the lumber onto the mill's ships.[12]

The records mention a church and a school, and it is likely that they were housed in one building. In 1889 there was also a guest house called the Rossin House, probably early inspiration for the France family—mill workers George and Wilfred, and their father Wilfred Sr.—who later established their own guest accommodations (Franceville House, and later Osborne House) midway down the Freddy Channel.

A prominent feature of early mill towns was the constant burning refuse pile, with its towering column of smoke visible for many miles. It was a noted feature of the mills at Waubaushene, Port Severn and Vic-

toria Harbour. However, Muskoka Mills had an additional method of handling its vast quantities of sawdust. There was a sawdust carrier, or spout, powered by water, which carried the sawdust up the heights to the east of the mills and into "a large trough-shaped waterway" destined for the neighbouring bay.[13]

It was in this manner that the infamous "sawdust bays," one to the west of the mills and the other to the east, in Clifton Bay, were created. (In 1884, the company was accused of environmental negligence for channelling the sawdust into fish spawning grounds.) More than a hundred years have passed and the sawdust is still many feet deep, despite the fact that much of it was used in early cottage days to insulate the ice in icehouses. Today, in addition to the acres of sawdust, the neat, low cairns of flat stone which supported the sawdust carrier can still be found immediately atop the heights, approximately seventy feet above the mill site. Numerous iron posts, which probably secured the carrier to the bluffs, also remain.

Arthur Norton, whose father was born and worked at Muskoka Mills, and whose aunt was drowned at an early age in the millrace, notes that when the mills finally closed his family relocated to Penetanguishene.

This was probably a typical move for millworkers following the closure of Muskoka Mills. It also seems likely that much of the machinery and even the buildings were sold to other mills or consumed by fire. Some of the village's houses burned in a legendary sawdust fire that smouldered underground for many years until it finally extinguished itself in 1910. Only a few bits and pieces remain of later buildings used by the caretaker who lived for many years on the site. It was probably his residency that caused mapmakers to show Muskoka Mills on their charts long after the lumber operation had ceased.

Pioneer Days

THE FIRST
COTTAGERS ARRIVE

Time present and time past
are both perhaps present in time future.
—T.S. Eliot

All Roads Lead to Georgian Bay

THERE WAS A TIME IN THE CENTURIES BEFORE THE FIRST cottagers arrived when the only route north from Lake Ontario was a well-worn aboriginal path that snaked up the Humber River to its head, overland in King Township, and down the West Holland River to Lake aux Claies (later named Lake Simcoe). From there intrepid travellers paddled to Barrie, trekked the Nine Mile Portage north and west of Kempenfeldt Bay (the present site of Barrie) overland to the Nottawasaga River, and finally headed down to Georgian Bay at Wasaga Beach.

In September 1793, Upper Canada's first lieutenant-governor, Sir John Graves Simcoe, set out to investigate this long and arduous route for himself. Travelling by horse and canoe, and in the company of various military men and native guides, Simcoe was determined to reach the shore of Georgian Bay. His interest in the route had less to do with creating recreational opportunities for settlers than with his emerging military strategy, which necessitated speedy access to a northern naval establishment. This was to be a back door for York and a refuge in the event of an attack from the south. Simcoe's report of this gruelling trip related that, "A gale of wind prevented my perfectly attaining this Object, but under the shelter of the Islands I went sufficiently close to satisfy myself, The Engineer and Surveyor, who accompanied me, that it was a safe and commodious Harbour, and capable of containing Vessels of as great Burthen as can be supposed to sail upon Lake Huron."[1]

Simcoe had found in Penetanguishene his ideal "back door," though it would be another two decades before his dream of a British military post there would be fully realized. Far less pleasing to the British army was the complicated voyage the route necessitated. So by year's end, Simcoe ordered the construction of Yonge Street, named for his friend and patron, Sir George Yonge, a late-eighteenth century British Secretary at War. In an effort to improve the difficult journey, he demanded that the street follow "as straight a line as possible"—an instruction well-heeded by Upper Canada's deputy surveyor, Augustus Jones, who routed it through and over just about any natural feature he encountered.[2]

It fell to Simcoe's soldiers, the men of the Queen's Rangers, to begin the monotonous process of clearing the sixty-five-foot-wide route with axes and oxen, and to lay lots on either side of the road for the settlers Simcoe

CAPTAIN BOXER OF THE ROYAL NAVY DREW THIS CARTOON IN 1845 AFTER SURVIVING A TRIP ON THE DIFFICULT PENETANGUISHENE ROAD.

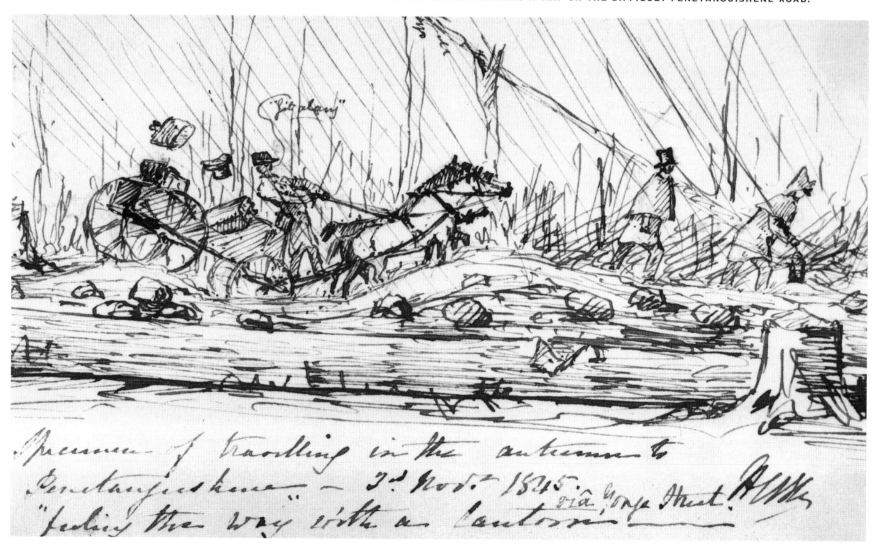

WIND, WATER, ROCK AND SKY

knew were necessary for future road maintenance.[3] By February 1796, the rough and muddy path connected midtown York with Lake Simcoe, where the road terminated at Holland Landing, fifty miles north of the fledgling town that was to become Toronto. It was a rooty, stump-infested thoroughfare for stagecoaches, but more importantly, just the connection Simcoe needed to the shores of Georgian Bay. In March of 1796, Mrs. Simcoe declared that "an Indian & a Canadian came [to York] from Matchadash [sic] Bay in five days, & said they could have travelled the journey in four."[4]

Nevertheless, there was still a great deal of work to be done on the world's longest street when Simcoe's role in its development came to an abrupt end. His perpetual ill-health finally got the better of him that summer and he returned with his family to England, leaving the monumental

THE WILLIAMS FAMILY CAMPED IN 1916, THE SUMMER ORVILLE WRIGHT RENTED THEIR COTTAGE, "WAUBEC."

task of road improvement in the hands of a group of mainly German settlers, who toiled to clear it in return for free land.[5]

It was laborious work, and the sometimes difficult relations between the settlers and government slowed it even further. It wasn't until 1825 that Yonge Street was finally extended north from Holland Landing through the forest to Kempenfeldt Bay, where it connected with a rough stretch of road leading directly to Penetanguishene. This second route followed an old native portage trail through the bush, one that had been expanded by the end of the War of 1812 to meet rising military needs. Penetanguishene Road, as it was called, became the main approach to the uninhabited land of the North Simcoe area and the shores of Georgian Bay.

Other roads soon began to appear, crisscrossing the country-

43

side and paving the way for settlement. In 1830, Coldwater Road replaced an old Indian trail running from the Narrows, near Orillia, to the Coldwater River, near Matchedash. Gloucester Road eased travel between Hillsdale and Matchedash Bay, Sunnidale Road improved access to the Nottawasaga from Kempenfeldt Bay, and Ridge Road opened up travel between Barrie and Orillia.

In 1853, transportation leaped ahead again, when the City of Toronto finished work on a railway that stretched from Lake Ontario to Barrie. By 1855, the Ontario, Simcoe and Huron Railway—the first passenger and freight service in Canada—was extended as far as Collingwood. The system, though a boon to travellers, was a financial failure until the government of Canada stepped in, refinanced it, renamed it The Northern, and handed it back to its original operators. By the time the 1870s were in full swing, travel by rail was all the rage. The Midland route, which originated in Port Hope, reached Midland in 1879, the same year the North Simcoe railway between Barrie and Penetanguishene was completed. Eventually, the various lines came together, first as part of the Grand Trunk and later the Canadian National system.

As a result of all this development the northland was rapidly opening up. Chunks of land were made available to settlers, sold by the government "on behalf" of the Chippewa Indians of Lakes Huron and Simcoe—with monies to benefit the displaced bands. Tourists and pioneer cottagers started visiting Cognashene in the late-nineteenth century, drawn by its spectacular scenery and recreational potential: hunting, fishing, boating, swimming. These early picnickers and campers (mostly residents of nearby Midland and Penetang) came during the summer months in small wooden launches, canoes, rowboats or sailboats. The winter landscape—with its uneven carpet of snowy shores and islands and windswept, frozen waters—was less welcoming to all but the hardiest of sportsmen.

By the turn of the century some campers travelled from as far afield as Collingwood, Thornbury and most impressively, Toronto. Despite the rail routes, this was a difficult trip in the pre-Highway 400 days. Once at their destination, they found themselves in uncharted territory, and so, unrestricted by official boundaries, campers and other visitors used the islands of Cognashene freely for the first few decades of the twentieth century.

The First Cottagers Arrive

THE HISTORY OF COGNASHENE AS COTTAGE COUNTRY BEGAN IN earnest in 1884 when Thomas Clark Street Macklem returned home to Canada from his studies at St. John's College, Cambridge. (He was later to become the Provost of Trinity College at the University of Toronto.) That summer he set sail in his *Lady Margaret* to navigate the still-uninhabited islands of the Georgian Bay with three of his university friends in tow, all of whom were named Arthur, curi-

AN OFFICIAL PORTRAIT OF THOMAS CLARK STREET MACKLEM (ABOVE LEFT), PAINTED DURING HIS TENURE AS PROVOST OF TRINITY COLLEGE. THE REVEREND T. CHARLES COCKING (LEFT) AND HIS WIFE MARION ETHEL (MINNIE) POSE DURING A VACATION IN THE ALPS. THE ORIGINAL STREET MACKLEM COTTAGE ON ARTHURS' ISLAND (RIGHT), FORMERLY KNOWN AS MINNEWAWA ISLAND.

THE BUSTLING PENETANG
STATION, WHERE EARLY
COTTAGERS CONNECTED WITH
CITY-BOUND TRAINS (AND
COGNASHENE-BOUND BOATS),
CAPTURED BY PROFESSIONAL
PHOTOGRAPHER J.W. BALD.

Transportation to Cognashene in the first decades of this century involved train travel to Penetang.

ously enough. They moored at various sites in the Cognashene area and camped ashore for a few days on the flat rocks at the north beach of what was then called Minnewawa Island.

Street Macklem was smitten. On his return to England, he began negotiating with the Department of Indian Affairs for the purchase of Minnewawa Island, along with the neighbouring Ogamog Island. The islands, being the first sold, are known as No. 1 and No. 2, and are described as lands which "are part and parcel of those set apart for the use of the Chippewas of Lakes Huron and Simcoe." The proceeds of the sale were to

THE BREITHAUPT'S BOAT (ABOVE). TOOLS
OF THE ICE-CUTTING TRADE (BELOW).

"be applied to the benefit, support and advantage of the said Indians."

The purchase was finally completed (for $80) in August 1885. Family tradition has it that when Street Macklem first visited the island after buying it, he was joined at his campfire by a native who remained silent for many

47

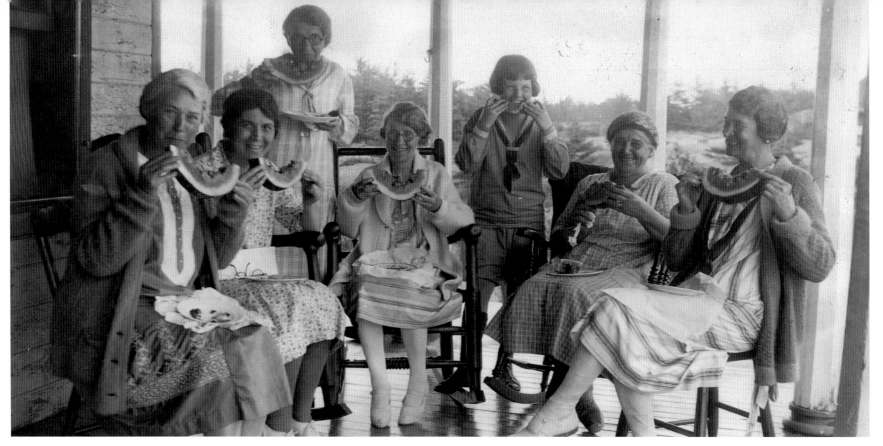

WHAT WOULD SUMMER AT THE COTTAGE BE WITHOUT WATERMELON AND FRIENDS WITH WHOM TO SHARE IT?

minutes before saying only that he was chief of the local tribe and that it had been his island before the Queen sold it. He then returned to his canoe and departed, a peaceful acknowledgement of the end of a way of life.

The original cottage on Arthurs' (No. 1) Island was probably built in 1885 and stood until 1927 when it burned to the ground and was replaced a year later. Little is known about the construction of this particular cottage, but it seems that concern about winter break-ins and theft in those early years prompted the family to empty it of its contents at the end of every summer. These were taken by scow back to Penetang and stored over the winter.

Soon enough, other pre-1900 cottages began to appear in Cognashene, including the Campbell cottage at Longuissa, the Williams' on Waubec and the Darling cottage at the northeast end of Townsend Is-

land. At the turn of the century, Charles Cocking, a Methodist minister in Penetang, bought the entire section of land from the Bluff, at the entrance to the north end of the Freddy Channel, to the Narrows at the entrance to Kaignashene Lake. It was a forty-acre parcel, though at the time Cocking believed it to be at least twice that size.

In 1900, the Cockings built two cottages, presently occupied by their great grandsons, and subdivided the rest of the land. These lots were soon sold to fellow ministers and friends. In the years between 1901 and 1910 a raft of cottages went up on the islands surrounding the Cockings'.

A GUEST AT BLARNEY CASTLE DEMONSTRATES HER DIVING TECHNIQUE IN 1920 (LEFT). JOHN MAHAFFY AND A GROUP OF FRIENDS ABOUT TO SET SAIL THE SAME YEAR (RIGHT).

Building a Cottage Life

OFTEN THE FIRST CONSTRUCTION on a newly acquired property was a wooden platform on which a tent could be erected; typically, the cooking took place outdoors. Almost all Cognashene cottagers started out this way and some continued to use tents for sleeping quarters even after a more permanent structure was built. Right into the 1990s many of the sites in Cognashene were tented on for several years before the first building was constructed, and to this day some people maintain platform tents to augment their sleeping accommodations.

The second permanent structure was usually a shed in which to store the tent and other equipment for the winter. Most lumber and building supplies were barged out from Midland or Penetang, though some were built of pine logs cut from trees on the site.

The first cottages were almost always positioned on the leeward side of the islands, looking east to the mainland. The exposed view to the open water was deemed unattractive and the gusting west wind was an unpleasant force to be avoided. The pine buildings were constructed with boards or logs of varying widths and left to darken with age. Extensive eaves were a popular feature that provided protection from the sun and rain. Bedrooms were usually diminutive—just large enough to hold a bed or a couple of bunks. Windows were also small and covered during the off-season with heavy shutters fastened with iron bars.

The abundant granite rock was commonly used for fireplaces and walkways around the grounds, but especially for the stone steps at doorways. When fire destroyed a cottage, the

A LAND RECEIPT AND TYPICAL EARLY COTTAGE CONSTRUCTION.

fireplace was usually the one remaining part of the original structure that could be incorporated into a new building.

The kitchen area was often housed in a separate but adjoining building in order to reduce the risk of fire and ensure as cool a cottage interior as possible. This also eliminated cooking odours in the living quarters, but meant that hot food had to be hustled across the open passage, cooling off considerably in the process. An ancillary bonus of this building arrangement: the kitchen could be accessed for emergency provisions by hunters or boaters stranded in the off-season. Several cottages in Cognashene still maintain separate kitchens.

Construction was usually a cooperative effort—*sans* local builder, just neighbours and friends pitching in. And as a result, there's no such thing as a "signature" Cognashene cottage. The look, if there is one, is highly individual. Built first and foremost to weather the elements, many of the earliest cottages have stood the test of time and today house fifth or sixth generation family members.

Early cottage life was not for the faint of heart—or weak of body. It was a complicated existence, full of sometimes difficult daily chores and challenges, things as basic today as the procuring and storing of fresh food. The modern refrigerator was still decades away. Icehouses were de rigueur. These small buildings were filled from the frozen waters each winter and often emptied before the summer's end. Fresh fish was a necessary staple and fortunately there was an endless supply. Wild strawberries, raspberries and blueberries were also plentiful and frequently rounded out the daily diet.

Word of the area's rough beauty was spreading, stimulating a modest tourist trade. Canadian and American visitors began vacationing at one of Cognashene's three summer hotels: Minnicognashene, Whalen's and Franceville. And like Street Macklem before them, many fell in love with the Bay and wound up buying their very own "piece of the rock."

Getting There was Half the Fun

TRANSPORTATION TO COGNASHENE IN THE FIRST DECADES OF THIS century involved train travel to Penetang (invariably a milk run, with much shunting of cars) and then a slow boat trip out to the islands. There were no cars back then, and even when they began to appear in the twenties, the roads were extremely rough. Most of the pioneer cottagers completed the trip in a day or two but the preparation took weeks; steamer trunks containing an entire summer's worth of supplies weren't easily prepared overnight.

ELINOR MEREDITH'S ACCOUNT OF A TYPICAL TRIP TO THE cottage, pre-1920s, suggests that it was for many (especially the children) a fantastic adventure, for others (presumably those responsible for the planning and pack-

ing), a tremendous amount of work:

Here was the happy realization of weeks of planning. A large steamer trunk was filled with carefully ironed sheets, pillowcases, table cloths,

(OPPOSITE, TOP LEFT) COTTAGING, CIRCA 1920, REQUIRED A CERTAIN AMOUNT OF SELF-SUFFICIENCY. (BELOW) MANY HANDS MAKE LIGHT WORK ON WASH DAY AT THE COOPER COTTAGE IN 1939, WITH EDWARD, ELEANOR, EDITH AND BARRY PITCHING IN. (THIS PAGE) A DAY-LONG PICNIC ORGANIZED BY THE SUTTONS AND THE BUTTS IN THE THIRTIES.

good Sunday "whites," and finally crammed shut. Dunnage bags were stuffed stiff with blankets, pillows and warm clothing. The whole load of some nine pieces of luggage was picked up by the horse-drawn CPR freight cart. Dressed in our best navy reefer coats and sailor collars, straw hats with streamers, white stockings, gloves, and black patent slippers for the girls, we youngsters were in an ecstasy of anticipation. With other cottage voyagers we trooped on the train and whirled around in our Pullman chairs. Great shunting of cars at Allandale, for some were off to Muskoka, and some to Penetang. 'There's the water, there is Georgian Bay!' On the water side of the dock panted the great ship Waubic in new paint, flags flying, gang plank laid out.

Time for work—get the 'launch' launched and started, the small boats prepared. What about the water system? Oh well, we can carry water, and mother knows how to make the old pump engine perform! Our jobs are to turn the water pump's big make-and-break wheel, cut off chunks of beautiful clear blue ice from the sawdust-covered blocks in our icehouse, and carry them to the ice box. We are in residence!

In sharp contrast, as one contemporary cottager points out, "Today, we arrive by supper, turn a key, flip a switch and we are in business!"

Hardship and Happy Times

EARLY COTTAGE LIFE REQUIRED EXTRA EFFORT AND enthusiasm on the part of the women. They had to be capable, adaptable and creative if they were going to make a success of summering in Cognashene. It was the wilderness, after all. It took a good deal of organizational skill just to ensure that all the provisions for a long season with extended family and guests would be on hand when needed.

COTTAGERS RELIED ON SUPPLY BOATS (ABOVE) TO DELIVER MUCH OF THEIR FOOD. FRESH FISH, ON THE OTHER HAND, WERE THERE FOR THE CATCHING.

52

A.Y. Jackson

EARLY SPRING, GEORGIAN BAY, 1920.

MARCH STORM, GEORGIAN BAY, 1920.

IN THE EARLY 1920S, COGNASHENE WAS the destination not only of campers and cottagers, but also of artists in search of inspiration. Chief among them was A.Y. Jackson and other members of the newly formed Group of Seven. Jackson wrote enthusiastically about the natural beauty of the area, but saved his most poignant tributes for the canvas. One year he wintered at Franceville and later recorded his impressions:

Georgian Bay has been one of my happy hunting grounds for camping and fishing at all seasons, and in all kinds of weath-er. Few people have seen it in wintertime and I had an urge to do so. In February 1920 I went to Penetang where I was forced by bad weather to stay for some days. When the weather cleared, I put on my snowshoes and headed for Franceville, fifteen miles away. Crossing the wide gap between the mainland and the islands I followed an old sleigh track. At Williams' Island where I had spent several summers I sat on the dock and fortified myself with a bar of chocolate. It was strange to see all frozen up and lifeless, the little bays and channels where I had paddled in summertime with various charming companions.

I received a very warm welcome at Franceville. The air was clear and sharp during my stay and it was generally sunny. On snowshoes I went in all directions and found so much material to paint that I used up all my panels and had to paint on the back

of them. We were almost isolated and seldom received any mail.

I amused the natives by carrying around with me a long pole in case I went through the ice. As the weather got milder, the ice got rotten and open water appeared. I had a little dinghy mounted on runners which I would pole over the ice; when I came to open water I would shove the dinghy in and take to the oars.

Later I painted up a number of canvases from sketches made that winter, among them "Freddy Channel" and "Cognashene Lake" and, now in the National Gallery, "Storm over a Frozen Lake" and "Early Spring."

TWO TRIPTYCHS PAINTED IN 1923, AFTER THE YOUNG ARTIST HAD WEATHERED A COGNASHENE WINTER.

MIDLAND'S MAIN STREET IN 1934 (ABOVE). CATALOGUES FOR ORDERING SUPPLIES (RIGHT) WERE A POPULAR CONVENIENCE FOR EARLY COTTAGERS.

The women learned to survive and thrive both because they had to and wanted to. The men came and went from the city on the weekends or on brief holidays during which they tended to the buildings and repairs. It was left to the women and children to haul the water, collect the wood, wash the clothes and bedlinens, and cook the meals—all in long dresses in the earliest days.

Laundry was a seemingly simple matter of washing the clothes at the water's edge and hanging them to dry on a sunny windy day. (Hot water was available only on cold days when the fireplace and wood stove were needed for heat.) Washtubs—which doubled as baths for children—and scrub boards are still used in a few cottages today. When electricity finally arrived, wringer-washers eased the chore to some extent, though often at the expense of damaged clothes and mangled fingers. It's surprising how often an old wringer-washer still turns up on the annual "large garbage" pick-up day.

Social life in the early cottage community was limited to the few neigh-

When electricity finally arrived, wringer-washers eased the chore to some extent, though often at the expense of damaged clothes and mangled fingers.

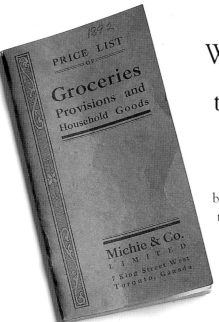

bours within rowing or swimming distance, often relatives or friends who had visited and then settled themselves. Picnics were popular from the start—so much so that many families reserved a special set of blackened pots for the occasion, along with pot holders, angle irons or grates to set the pots on, and a basket for the enamel plates. Fishing, swimming and berry picking were always a prominent part of these all-day events.

Although the rocks and water yielded plenty of fish, ice, berries, and wood in the early years, the matter of other fresh food items was more complicated. A variety of supply boats from the mainland served Cognashene for many years, operating on a more or less regular schedule. Weather permitting, they would stop at one of the area's large docks, where cottagers converged by canoe, rowboat or sailboat to collect their orders.

Later, the T. Eaton Company accepted large orders from summer cottagers and delivered dry goods to the landing at Penetang in time to accompany families out to their cottages at the start of the season. Eventually a store was built at Whalen's, where cottagers—and teenagers especially—gathered daily during the week to meet the *Midland City* en route to Parry Sound, and later, the *Penetang Eighty-Eight* on its way up to Wawataysee. These big passenger and supply boats delivered mail as well as fresh meat and bread.

The *Midland City* steamship also provided a means for midweek shopping in Midland, collecting passengers at Whalen's midmorning and returning them from town mid-afternoon. Longtime cottager Marion Bowden once recalled what a scramble this could be:

Who can ever forget the frantic rush uptown, the big shopping decisions to be hurriedly made, with usually little or no time for lunch in town?

The local stores were most obliging in delivering purchases to the dock, but it was a lucky day when a housewife went back to her own cottage with all her own provisons.

How many times we rushed down the main street at 1:50 p.m. for the 2 o'clock departure, only to sit on deck while awaiting the arrival of the train from Toronto. Sometimes it could be a long wait, especially on a hot day, until the train steamed in and the loading and unloading began.

AS DIFFERENT AS THE EARLY COTTAGE EXPERIENCE WAS, WITH ITS lack of electricity, transportation, communication and technology, some fundamental things haven't changed. The wind-battered pines, rugged islands, often treacherous waters, the ever-threatening storms, and the barren terrain endure forever. They're what drew the first pioneers to the area, full of awe and expectation, and they continue to draw us still.

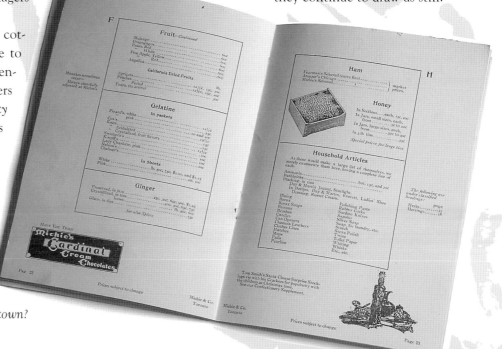

GETTING THERE

SHIPS AND BOATS AND FLOATING THINGS

IT IS NEARLY IMPOSSIBLE TO OVERSTATE THE IMPORTANCE OF boats among the islands of Cognashene. There can be few areas in the province—in North America, for that matter—where such a sizeable community is so dependent upon water transportation. Cottagers rely on them to get to their cottages, to visit neighbours, to collect supplies and mail, and it must be admitted, sometimes just for fun.

Boats are as inextricably linked to the local history and development as they are to the convenience and comfort of cottagers today. That said, such complete dependence on water transportation can, in fact, be a colossal *inconvenience* at times—one which leaves travellers at the mercy of the weather. But ask any Cognashener, and he or she will probably tell you they wouldn't have it any other way. Because the very bane of their existence is also an enviable source of pleasure and pride, and very likely the key to the quiet isolation the islanders still experience from time to time.

The Early Days: The Steamers

THE ARRIVAL OF COMMERCE ON THE SHORES OF GEORGIAN Bay necessitated the introduction of steamer ships to convey supplies and workers to the lumber mills and other businesses, and later to ferry early tourists and cottagers to their otherwise inaccessible destinations.

Bay's northeast shore. Penetang was her main port of call, where she connected with north and southbound trains and departed daily at 2:15 in the afternoon. Her first stop was at the dock of the Royal Hotel in Honey Harbour, from whence she made her way to the Hotel Minnicognashene, Whalen's, Go Home Bay, Wawataysee and so on, up to Parry Sound, carrying passengers, mail, baggage and freight. For the return trip, she left Parry Sound bright and early at 7 a.m. and arrived at about noon at Penetang, just in time to meet the train bound for Toronto.

The *Waubic* completed this run every day from 1911 (when she was brand-new) to 1920 inclusive. She was a twin-screw vessel—the first to grace this route—with spacious passenger decks, meal service, and ten or so cabins to accommodate passengers staying overnight. She was nearly 135 feet long and twenty-five feet wide, with an average speed of sixteen miles per hour. Her captain, the legendary John "Punch" Dubé, and all of her officers sported smart blue uniforms, while

In the 1880s, George Dubé ran the *Equal Rights* and the *Home Rule* out of Penetang. By the next decade, Captain Billy France and his brother George had purchased the *Home Rule* and proceeded to use her for a number of their enterprises, including the family's hotel at Franceville. By 1900, the *John Lee* was making regular runs from Penetang, where she would meet the train and then transport passengers and supplies to Honey Harbour, Tomahawk, Minnicog, Whalen's and Franceville. Later, she would also stop at the Cockings, one of the first families to establish a cottage in Cognashene. Eventually, the *John Lee* was relocated to the Parry Sound area, where she burned in about 1913.

In Cognashene, she was replaced for one or two years by a yacht called the *Electric*, which had formerly been used as a private yacht on Lake Ontario until she was converted for commercial use on Georgian Bay. At the same time—and until the late twenties—the *Trader* and then the *City Queen*, two smaller steamers, saw service in the area as passenger and supply boats. The *City Queen* had a reputation for being a bit of a *grande dame* which sank more than once when her leaks became unmanageable.

The *Waubic* was probably the finest and largest ship ever to serve the island communities along Georgian

THE *CITY QUEEN* (ABOVE). THE *WAUBIC* AWAITS HER PASSENGERS AT THE PENETANG DOCK (BELOW).

The Vancrofter

THOUGH WELL-EQUIPPED IN OTHER WAYS, THE VANCROFTER WAS MOTORLESS AND HAD TO BE TOWED FROM PLACE TO PLACE AROUND THE BAY.

THE *VANCROFTER* WAS A HOUSE-boat originally owned by the Van-crofters, an American family, who kept the large boat in Parry Sound. As was the case with other similar houseboats of the day, the *Vancrofter* was built on a large scow and had to be towed from place to place on the water. The tug owner hired by the Van-crofters to tow it around Georgian Bay was owed a considerable amount of money for his services, and had already seized the houseboat when Louis Jacob Breithaupt took an interest

in it and bought it in 1908 for $950.

The *Vancrofter* was fully furnished and almost unbelievably well-equipped. It could sleep twenty-five people, had plumbing and hand pumps, and was wired for plugging in at any convenient dock. It was a regular floating cot-tage, and it satisfied the family until 1912, when Louis Jacob purchased Island 94 and christened it "Chippewa Island."

The Breithaupts continued to use the house-boat for a number of years, having it towed from place to place around the southern shore of

Georgian Bay. It would be one of the last of its kind to remain afloat (others already lay grounded on Keating Island), thanks largely to the family's tender loving care. They were care-ful to caulk it each spring prior to using it, how-ever eventually—inevitably—the *Vancrofter* sprung a leak. While no serious damage was sus-tained, Mrs. Breithaupt insisted that it be hauled up on the family's land, where it still stands today (though both the island and the houseboat now belong to the Simpsons), a curi-ous reminder of an earlier cottage era.

the ship itself was what one cottager remembers as "nautically correct" with its neatly coiled ropes, deep-throated whistle, and clouds of black smoke billowing from her stacks.

After 1921, she was removed from the waters of Georgian Bay for good when her owners declared her too costly to operate. She would be quickly replaced, but never again would Cognashene see a vessel as fast or as glamourous as the *Waubic*.

The *Midland City* brought a different kind of romance to the waters of Cognashene. She arrived as a side-wheeler in 1920, trailing great plumes of black smoke that would billow from her smokestacks when her steam-engine boilers were fired, and she would announce her presence with long blasts on her powerful steam whistle.

To travel on the *Midland City* in those days was to travel in style: there was a restaurant on the aft deck, staterooms for the well-to-do, and a large staff that included deckhands, a purser, an engineer, firemen, a chef, kitchen staff, waitresses and chambermaids.

MD4   STEAMER "MIDLAND CITY" 30,000 ISLANDS. GEORGIAN BAY. ONT., CANADA

Thus equipped, the handsome *Midland City* served the area for thirty years, bringing cottagers, baggage, building supplies, general freight, grocery orders and mail to Whalen's landing and other points north.

But the stately steamship was no spring chicken. She was already fifty years old when she first came to the Bay. Originally built in Glasgow in 1870, she was shipped in sections to Kingston, where she was reassembled at the Davis shipyards and launched on August 16, 1871, as the *Maud*, after a daughter of her first owner, Charles Gildersleeve. She originally measured 120-by-32 feet and drew only three or four feet of water, but from

1894 to 1895 she was enlarged, mostly in length, and renamed the *America*. In 1920, the Georgian Bay Tourist Company of Midland brought the 553-ton ship to the Bay, renamed her the S.S. *Midland City* and launched her at Midland. (Her predecessor, the *Waubic*, had run out of Penetang, so the change in port highlighted the fact that Midland would henceforth be the southern terminus for the overnight Parry Sound run.)

Her time in the Bay was to prove eventful. In the mid-twenties, she suffered the indignity of sinking while moored at her pier in Midland. During a thunderstorm, the water level dropped suddenly, the guardrail of the boat caught on the dock, and the *Midland City* tipped on her side. Her portholes, which had been left open for ventilation, quickly filled with water and the boat flooded. Eventually, the water was pumped out, but not before she had spent some time resting on the bottom.

On August 26, 1934, on a return run to Midland after picking up passengers in Go Home Bay and Cognashene, she struck a shoal off Present Island. The captain, realizing the boat was sinking fast, put her "full steam ahead" and was able to beach the *Midland City* on the sandy bottom of Midland Point. It was a calm day and there were no casualties, but it was a close call—the stern deck was underwater by the time it was all over.

And then in the late forties, the engines of the *Midland City* suddenly and inexplicably gave out in the midst of a heavy blow, south of O'Donnell Point. It was only after several very nervous moments, with the waves spouting geysers off the nearby rocks, the boat drifting swiftly and helplessly, and

To travel on the *Midland City* in those days was to travel in style.

a petrified passenger pounding out "Nearer My God to Thee" on the ship's third-deck piano, that the engines finally restarted and the *Midland City* continued on to Copperhead.

In 1955, the register of the *Midland City* was closed for good. The fact that she was no longer able to meet safety standards was merely the straw that broke the camel's back. Tourists and cottagers had speedier and more dependable boats of their own by then, and the need for such a craft was so severely diminished that its operation was no longer viable. The contents were auctioned off and the hulk pulled up on shore, near where the Wye Heritage Marina now stands. What was not of value was burned or

THE *CITY OF DOVER* CAME TO THE BAY IN 1928 AND WAS OPERATED AS LATE AS 1960.

left to rot. At the time she was "de-registered," she was said to be the oldest commercial vessel of this type operating in North America.

In 1928, the *City of Dover* was pressed into service by the Georgian Bay Tourist Company to augment the *Midland City*'s operations. At seventy-four feet she was a smaller vessel, but for over twenty years she saw daily service through Cognashene to Go Home Bay, returning to Midland via Honey Harbour. For a few seasons, she ran as far north as Pointe au Baril.

She was sold in 1955 for service on Lake Superior, but returned the following summer and made occasional runs as late as 1960. At that point she was discovered to have a cracked keel, a prohibitively expensive prob-

lem to repair. Plans to convert her into a floating dance hall on the Severn River were abandoned in the face of stiff fire regulations, and eventually she was pulled up on the shore and left to the elements.

The service provided by the *Midland City* was never really replaced, but for almost fifteen years ending in 1968 the *Penetang Eighty-Eight* (later named the *Midland Penetang Eighty-Eight*) would bring tourists on sightseeing excursions through the area and would also carry groceries, supplies and mail to Whalen's. The *Eighty-Eight* was due there daily at 3 p.m., and just about everybody in Cognashene (or so it seemed) would turn out to meet the boat, collect the mail and do a little shopping and visiting. When the *Eighty-Eight* stopped running, the community lost one of its most treasured and unifying traditions.

THE *EIGHTY-EIGHT* WAS A FAIRMILE, a vessel originally designed for military service by the Fairmile Motor Boat Company in the U.K. During the Second World War hundreds of such boats were built around the world for the Allied war effort. They were used primarily, although not exclusively, for near-shore ocean patrols and submarine-hunting. Several of these boats were built at the Port Carling Boat Works in Honey Harbour where the Honey Harbour Boat Club is now situated. Others in the Ontario program were built in Midland, Orillia and Toronto.

The *Eighty-Eight* was built in 1942 or 1943 at J.J. Taylor & Son in Toronto. After the war, she was mothballed along with others of her class at Sorel, Quebec. Bill Christie, who would later became a Cognashene cottager, wrote to the federal government offering to purchase one of the surplus vessels for $1,000. He received an indignant reply to the effect that the ships had cost close to $250,000 to build and outfit, and they scoffed at his paltry offer. Christie upped the ante to $2,000, and was again rebuffed—however, this time they informed him that for another two thousand, he could have his pick of the fleet!

And so it was that the *Eighty-Eight* (the number signified its commission for wartime service) made her way to Toronto, sailed up the St. Lawrence by Christie and some chums. There she was refitted for use as a pleasure

THE *PENETANG EIGHTY-EIGHT* HAD A LONG AND ILLUSTRIOUS CAREER, STARTING IN WORLD WAR II AND ENDING AT GANANOQUE.

boat, complete with a master stateroom and flush toilets. In 1947, Christie brought the boat to Penetang and used her to explore the north shore. Six years later he sold her to Pete LePage of Penetang, who was the first to put her to use as a commercial vessel. In addition to Cognashene, the *Eighty-Eight* serviced Go Home Bay, Wawataysee and, for a while, Manitou.

After 1968, she was used near Gananoque as a training vessel for sea cadets, until she sank one spring after a log pierced her hull. Efforts to refloat her were unsuccessful and the *Eighty-Eight* now lies undisturbed in her watery grave.

A New Era of Boating

IN SHARP CONTRAST TO THE GRAND STEAMERS AND LARGE COMmercial vessels that once plied Cognashene's waters, the first motorized boats owned by cottagers would today be considered "putt-putts." It's hardly a dignified description. The small, open boats had very little deck and

in many respects resembled a Mackanaw (a popular fishing-cum-pleasure boat built in Collingwood and other spots around the Bay) without the sails. Typically, the steering wheel would be mounted on the side of the boat, with the steering handle driving a rudder with the aid of ropes and pulleys. The engine was mounted midships.

Speed was never the point of these early boats, which were often used to tow other boats—canoes, rowboats, etc.—to picnics. Though there was once a race in conjunction with the annual regatta, the dangerous practice was discontinued when a passenger fell out of the boat and was injured by a rotating propeller.

While the trend in the last few decades has been toward serviceable fibreglass boats designed to withstand the elements, there remains a strong sense of attachment in the community to the wooden boats of earlier days. This fascination is reflected in organized "sail pasts" of classic, gleaming wooden boats—events that formally celebrate their undeniable beauty and rightful place in the annals of cottaging.

LONGUISSA WHALEN'S

BLARNEY CASTLE —

— MINNICOGNASHENE

CHURCH ON THE ROCKS

SPECIAL PLACES

WHALEN'S FRANCEVILLE

LONGUISSA WHALEN'S

BLARNEY CASTLE —

— MINNICOGNASHENE

CHURCH ON THE ROCKS

LONGUISSA

A RICH HISTORY OF HOSPITALITY

WHEN A GROUP OF BUSINESS ASSOCIATES CAME TOGETHER to form the Muskoka Mill & Lumber Company in 1875, it was in an effort to revive the mill previously operated by the ambitious and imprudent Anson Dodge. Among the associates were Anson's own father, William Dodge, and one Archibald Hamilton Campbell, a man who brought a wealth of varied experience to the endeavour.

Archibald was born in 1819 near Stirling, Scotland. He was the youngest and possibly most ambitious son of the Campbells of Carbrook. By the tender age of twenty-six, Archibald had already dabbled in the classics, banking and law. But like others of his age, he was discouraged by the bleak economic outlook in the British Isles and left home in 1845 to seek his fortune in Canada, a young and largely undeveloped country.

Following his arrival in Ontario, the versatile Scotsman applied himself to both the mining and banking industries before returning home to Carbrook for a visit in 1856. It was during this trip that he had the good fortune to meet Louisa Fisher of Dunkeld, a spirited young woman whose taste for adventure apparently matched Archibald's own. The pair wasted little time in marrying, and with his bride by his side, Archibald returned to Ontario and settled for a number of years in Kingston.

It was in Peterborough, where the Campbells moved next, that Archibald was introduced to the lumber industry as co-owner (with Amer-

At the turn of the century, a two-storey cottage—Longuissa—stood solidly

ican partners) of the Nassau Mills, situated on the Otonabee River where Trent University stands today. The property included 100 acres on either side of the winding river, and the mills, which were among the largest in Upper Canada at the time. In 1866 alone, the Nassau Mills produced ten million board feet of sawn lumber—twenty per cent of the entire output of Peterborough County.

Although the mill thrived for a time, the Peterborough years were not happy ones for the couple, who suffered the devastating loss of three of their young children. (Of the nine children Louisa eventually bore, six would survive.) This tragic turn of events, coupled with the decline in business caused by the recession at the end of the American Civil War, prompted Archibald and his partners to sell the lumber business and look to Georgian Bay for their future.

While Archibald settled into his work at the Muskoka Mills, he moved his young family to Toronto, a city of growing prosperity and comparative

comfort. The couple decided to build a home on the southwest corner of Bloor Street and Avenue Road, one of the city's more prestigious address-es, and in a nostalgic gesture named it Carbrook, after the Campbell home in Scotland. (The house was later torn down to make way for the Royal Ontario Museum.) In the summer of 1877, the same year that Carbrook was completed, Louisa gave birth to Muriel, her ninth and last child.

Amy (the Campbell's second-youngest daughter), who faithfully record-ed the family's comings and goings in her diaries, painted a vivid picture of Toronto life at the end of the nineteenth century. For the Campbell ladies, it was a social time full of tea parties, theatre, churchgoing, chari-ties, weddings, visiting, and of course, receiving guests at home. It isn't dif-ficult to imagine that the tradition of hospitality which was later at the heart of Longuissa was nurtured in the Campbell children during this time.

In January 1887, Archibald, whose holdings in the mills had increased by this time, paid $100 to the Muskoka Mill & Lumber Company for lots

on the hill overlooking the Bay, constructed of top-grade Campbell timber.

40 and 41, Concession 6 of Gibson Township. They were part of the peninsula dividing the long and narrow Longuissa Bay from the mouth of the Musquash River. Within six months, a two-storey cottage—Longuissa—stood solidly on the hill overlooking the Bay, constructed of top-grade pine from the Campbell timber rights. Its interior was, and is, a showcase of innovative craftsmanship—the quality of the wood best displayed where narrow strips are laid diagonally for effect. French doors lead from the first-floor living room to the generous verandah with its magnificent view. Upstairs, a splendid second-floor gallery surrounds and overlooks the main floor. One of the first-ever skylights is constructed above it, and beneath is the long dining-room table which used to seat as many as twenty-five people, and is still in use today. The kitchen is separately housed, as was often the custom at that time.

Of the cottage's many handsome features, the ones which catch every visitor's eye are the whimsical, hand-carved wooden panels created—with much humour—by daughter Frances and her friends. "Abandon care all ye who enter here" is sound advice to all visitors, but *"Pas d'elle yeux Rhone cas nous"* is the epigram which has always challenged observers most.

From 1887 on, names of family members and guests were duly recorded in the Longuissa visitors' books, a series of leather-bound volumes still found in the cottage today. From the beginning, the Campbells and their six children were there, and even that first year there were seventeen guests, some of whom would return many times over the years.

Once again, Amy's colourful diaries are a treasure trove of information about the early days at Longuissa. Not surprisingly, picnics were the most popular pastime, invariably consisting of hard-boiled eggs, meat, bread, jam and pots of hot tea. One or two canoes would be paddled ahead to the designated spot where a fire was started, while everyone else, including Mrs. Campbell, would arrive later. Many of the family's favourite picnic destinations are still popular today: the cottages below the tennis court, at

the Sandy Beach, near the Point in Brown's Bay, at the Last Resort, at Three Rocks, at Bone Island Point, at the Shingle Mill, through the Freddy Channel past Cognashene to the Open, the Lizard or Eshpabekong. Generally, weather determined the choice of location.

REST AND RELAXATION HAD THEIR PLACE AT LONGUISSA, but it is more often recalled as a centre of intense activity. In many ways, it was a bit like summer camp, with plenty of activities to choose from and no shortage of companions with whom to play. Walking was popular and vigorous back then, and would often fill an entire afternoon, but the rewards made the effort worthwhile: white orchids and sweet-smelling yellow flowers from the swamp up the Freddy Channel, bergamot, and black-eyed Susans or gentians at the Shingle Mill. Sometimes the rewards were edible, as there were blueberries and raspberries galore.

Fishing, too, was a popular sport, as was tennis, and Longuissa boasted the first wooden court on Georgian Bay. While the surface has changed over the years, it remains in constant use.

In the early years, getting to Longuissa from Toronto was an all-day journey. Visitors took a train to Allandale, transferred to a two-car "local" to Penetang and would be met by a boat for the fifteen-mile voyage over the water to Longuissa. Later, the *Midland City* would deposit visitors at Minnicog or Whalen's where they would be met by someone from the house, perhaps in the disappearing propeller boat, or in a long rowboat with two sets of oars. Later, it might have been the *Seaway*, the Longuissa launch.

While the Campbells were in residence, the Visitors' books were full of the names of businessmen and educators, clergymen and bishops, lawyers, judges and architects, a veritable "who's who" of Ontario society. But in 1894, a new name appeared in the book—that of Leighton Goldie McCarthy—and it appeared each year until his death in 1952. Six years after his first visit to the cottage, Leighton and Muriel were married quietly at Toronto's St. James Cathedral with just their immediate

THE WARM, RICH WOOD INTERIOR OF THE COTTAGE'S LIVING ROOM GIVES WAY TO THE GENEROUS FRONT PORCH (OPPOSITE), WHERE LOUISA USED TO SIT EVERY EVENING AND WATCH THE SUN GO DOWN. ONE OF FRANCES' FAMOUS EPIGRAMS IS ABOVE THE FRENCH DOORS. THE CUPBOARD (ABOVE) LOOKS MUCH THE SAME TODAY AS IT WOULD HAVE A CENTURY AGO. THE TRUNK (LEFT), INSCRIBED WITH THE MUSKOKA MILL & LUMBER COMPANY LOGO, IS FILLED WITH OLD, BUT PERFECTLY PRESERVED, LINENS AND OTHER HOUSEHOLD TREASURES.

Though his trips to the Bay were infrequent, Leighton cherished the peace that they offered.

families present. Their daughter Leigh was born the next year and taken to the Bay in the summer of 1901. Zina followed in 1904, Nancy in 1907, Jean (affectionately known as Jummie) in 1908, and John in 1913. All of the children were introduced to the Bay as babies.

IN 1909, WHEN ARCHIBALD CAMPBELL PASSED AWAY IN HIS NINETIETH year, Toronto and Georgian Bay lost a prominent friend and citizen. Longuissa passed to his wife, Louisa, and upon her death, to their eldest daughter, Frances. In 1918, Leighton bought Longuissa for Muriel, and in doing so opened another chapter in its long history.

Leighton had been raised in Barrie, the son of a country doctor and the eldest of five children. Called to the bar at the age of twenty-two, he went on to represent the riding of North Simcoe as a federal member of parliament for ten years. Leighton later earned a reputation as one of Canada's top corporate lawyers and was appointed to the position of director, then solicitor and eventually president of the Canada Life Assurance Company. In addition, he was president of the National Trust Company, chairman of the Toronto Savings and Loan Company, and a director of many other companies. With his brother Frank, his cousin D.L. McCarthy, and others, he formed the partnership which became the noted Canadian law firm of McCarthy and McCarthy (McCarthy Tetrault today).

During these busy years, Muriel spent her summers with their children at Longuissa. Nurses and a governess would accompany her when the children were young, but it was Muriel who really ran the Good Ship Longuissa. She was captain, navigator, social coordinator, sports director and chaplain all rolled into one energetic package. "My mother was fantastic," recalled Jummie. "She entertained mobs of young people all summer."

With his hectic work schedule, Leighton's trips to the Bay were infrequent, but he cherished the peace that they offered.

LOUISA AND ARCHIBALD CAMPBELL (AT LEFT), AMY STANDING IN THE REAR, FRANCES (RIGHT, SEATED ON THE ROCK), AND MURIEL IN THE FOREGROUND.

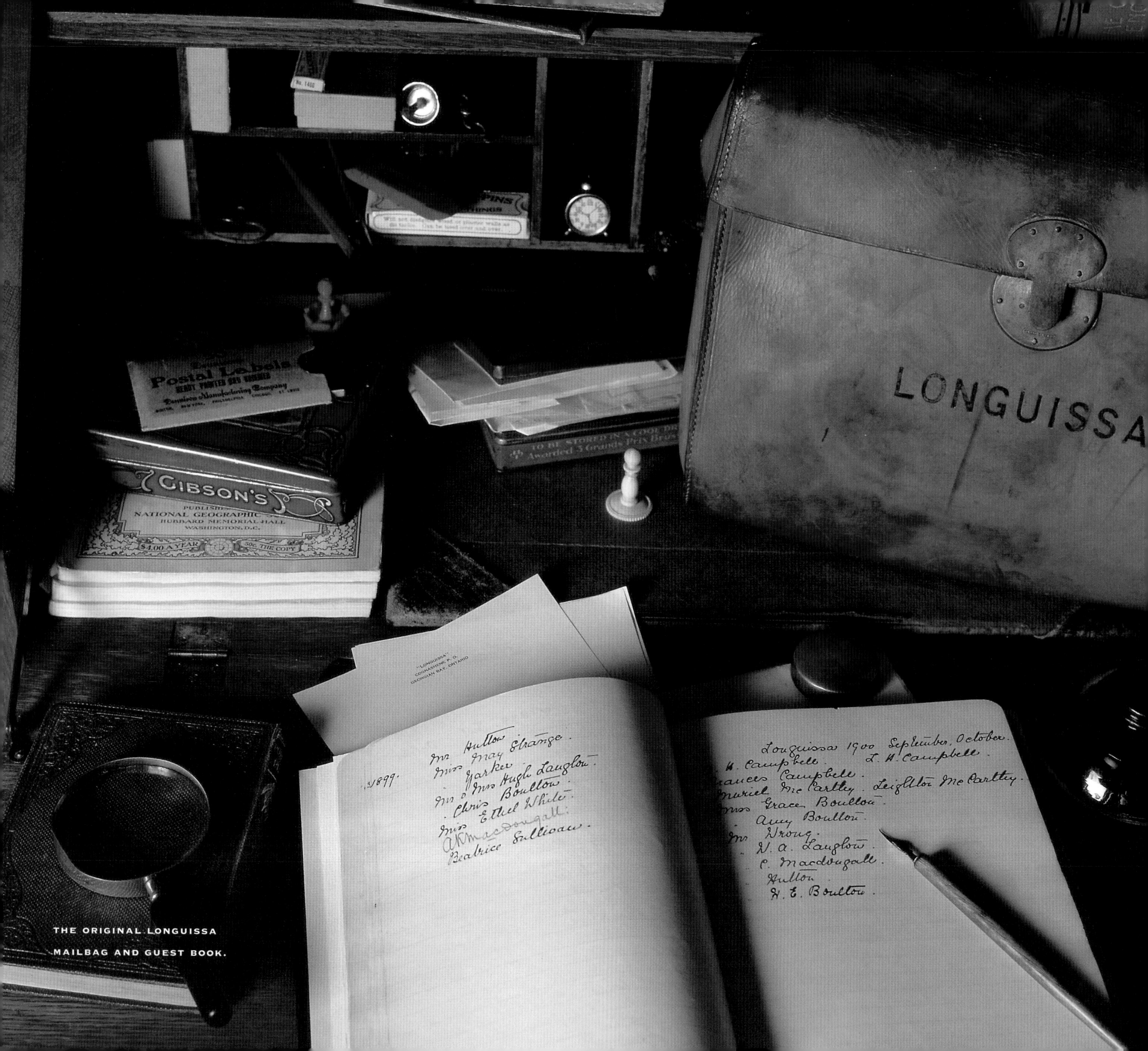

THE ORIGINAL LONGUISSA MAILBAG AND GUEST BOOK.

A Day in the Life of Longuissa

AT 8:30 A.M. A GONG SIGNALLED the first skinny-dip of the day. Fortunately, the girls had their own area with an ingenious "privacy set-up." After a quick change in the bathhouse they emerged wrapped in towels and ran to a large box-like structure—four-sided and open to the sky. While hidden from prying eyes, the girls slipped into the water and emerged outside the box, discreetly hidden under the waves. The

boys—having been given the all-clear signal—would proceed to swim behind the bathhouse. It was a sad day when the old building finally had to be taken down.

Breakfast was at 9 a.m., following morning prayers. Porridge and fruit juice would be served on the verandah and then came a feast of scrambled eggs, bacon, kidneys, liver, fish and toast, which John McCarthy still recalls. Someone

had the chore of paddling to Franceville to get the fresh milk. Others would prepare for the picnic—building the fire, preparing the food or helping with the washing up. After lunch Muriel would read aloud from the current novel—a story that might last several weeks. As Terence Cronyn, a master at Ridley College and a frequent visitor, once observed, "The continuity was not easy to maintain, as one often fell asleep before the end of the chapter." On returning to the cottage from a picnic, tennis, swimming, walking, or boating were the next activities of choice.

Dinner was at 7:30 sharp and everyone was expected to dress for it, the women in dresses and the men in white flannels, blazers and ties. Afterward, there were games—cards, checkers, rummy—and the young might go canoeing or have a bonfire where songs were inevitably sung. "A goldfish swam in a big glass bowl" was Muriel's favourite; "I know a happy land where drinks abound" tickled John's fancy; and "I'll be loving you" was Jummie's husband's favourite. At 10:30 p.m., a horn would sound and all would retire for the night.

Muriel's days always began early. It was she who wrote the daily orders for Wilf France, who travelled to Penetang to shop for the cottagers. Given Wilf's peculiar schedule, his delivery might be as late as midnight, in which case family or servants would be in the kitchen unpacking groceries at 1 o'clock in the morning. Mail, too, was looked after by Wilf, an important duty as all visitors had to receive a written invitation from Muriel.

Muriel loved Longuissa, but it was probably the months before and after the heat and bustle of the summer that were her favourite times. She would entertain a few friends, clear trails, and take long walks. Occasionally she would stay on until the snow fell.

LEIGHTON MCCARTHY AND FRANKLIN ROOSEVELT AT WARM SPRINGS, GEORGIA. ROOSEVELT SIGNED THE PICTURE AND
SENT IT TO HIS FRIEND WITH THE INSCRIPTION, "LEIGHTON—HUNGRY?"

There are several significant parallels in the favourite pastimes of the summer home's two principal families. Both the Campbells and the McCarthys considered the enthusiastic participation of family and friends to be a vital part of life at Longuissa. And both families extended countless invitations to guests from all over Canada and the United States. One of the many distinguished visitors to Longuissa was the Right Honourable Vincent Massey, Canada's first Canadian-born Governor General. In *What's Past is Prologue: The Memories of Vincent Massey* he reminisced about his visits to the Bay in 1911 and 1912.

I spent some very happy holidays in Georgian Bay where friends of mine had a house known widely as "Longuissa." The establishment was really a matriarchy, with our hostess, Mrs. Archibald Campbell, presiding over it, following traditions that have disappeared long since. Longuissa had a routine— inflexible, even monumental. Some of it was inherited from Scotland, some of it belonged to Canada. At breakfast, porridge was consumed peripatetically—all of us moving slowly about the verandah. This habit has long since disappeared (you can't eat Corn Flakes moving around). Chaperonage was unshaken. If we were gathered in the evening and two young people were miss-

ing, their absence would be noted by our hostess and commented on. Lunch took place on an island or a point some distance away from the house—a delicious cold meal, at which everyone was required to choose an implement (never two, still less three), knife or fork or spoon; no more. In addition to the hampers for lunch, there was always a basket for books—the book you happened to be reading, or some spares, and always Blackwood's and The Cornhill. In due course, we would return to the house and engage in whatever activity we wished—or almost what we wished. Our hostess and her family were determined that the house party at Longuissa should not be disturbed by invasion. If anyone was so ill-advised as to pay an impromptu visit to the family, whoever saw them approaching would sound the alarm and the entire family and guests would disappear from the house into the adjoining woods. The visitors might well be intimate friends in Toronto, but the friendship was not exportable. No motorboats were permitted in the bay; no irritating noise from engines; no gasoline fumes.

I N 1943, SHORTLY BEFORE LEIGHTON became Canada's first ambassador to the United States, another distinguished statesman visited Georgian Bay—President Franklin Delano Roosevelt. It was wartime, of course, and like a complicated military manoeuvre, Leighton's plans for the President's fishing holiday required the utmost secrecy. After the trip was over a grateful Roosevelt wrote as follows:

My dear Leighton,
Thanks to you, all of the arrangements for my recent Canadian visit were everything that I had hoped for. We had the usual variety of fishing luck; but on the whole most excellent sport and many pleasant days on the water in your beautiful country. I hope that you will be good enough to express my thanks to everyone for their tact and kindness enabling me to have a truly restful week. I am particularly conscious of the many preparations made by the Canadian Pacific Railroad officials and the excellent and efficient services rendered me by the Canadian Mounted Police—the representatives who were assigned to my train fully upheld the fine reputation of that splendid body.

Thank you ever so much for your thoughtfulness and kindness.
Cordially yours, Franklin D. Roosevelt

I N JANUARY 1945, WITH THE SECOND WORLD WAR NEARING AN end, Leighton resigned as ambassador. He returned to Canada and was replaced in Washington by Lester B. Pearson. When Roosevelt died at Warm Springs, Georgia, a few months later, his old friend Leighton was by his side. In October 1952, Leighton himself passed away at Longuissa, three years after his beloved Muriel had died.

In the forty-five years since Leighton's death, the Longuissa tradition has been well-nurtured and maintained. The summer home has been continuously occupied by Leighton's descendants: initially, by each of his and Muriel's five children, and subsequently by their children and grandchildren. Today, Longuissa is occupied by the daughters of Leighton's third eldest daughter (Nancy Manners Bell) and their children, the fifth generation of the original Campbell family to spend their summers at Longuissa.

When, on a warm summer day in 1987, more than seventy descendants of the famously private Campbell/McCarthy clan gathered to celebrate the cottage's 100th anniversary, they did so in typical Longuissa style: a picnic at noon on Longuissa Point followed by an evening dinner party. And when, at the end of the day, the family stood together on the verandah where so many generations of family pictures had been taken, it was with a profound sense of belonging and nostalgia.

Now into its second century, the cottage remains a treasured family home. At its heart lie the fascinating traditions initiated by the Campbells, preserved by the McCarthys and perhaps best expressed by Elizabeth Bell (fourth generation) who, since birth, has spent a part of every summer at Longuissa:

Love, loyalty, laughter, learning and leisure
Optimism, old, time-honoured traditions tempered by the present
Narratives, nieces, nephews and cousins as neighbours
Guidance, gentleness, giving, growing up
Unity of family, uniqueness, understanding
Inspiration, imagination, insights, inner journeys
Strength of character, self-reliance, sharing, sense of humour, songs, smiles
Solitude, serenity, spirituality, 'soul' food
Acceptance, anticipation, artistry, personal awakening.

FRANCEVILLE

AN INDELIBLE IMPRESSION

TOWARD THE END OF THE NINETEENTH CENTURY THE Canadian Pacific Railway mounted an advertising campaign in Britain. Their objective was to promote Canada, the land of opportunity, and they tempted potential immigrants with the promise of cheap land and plentiful work. Wilfred and Susannah France were probably typical of those who responded to the advertisements and brochures: resourceful, working-class English and Scottish stock.

Still, it was a courageous step in 1887 when the couple said goodbye to their family and friends in Sheffield, Yorkshire, and set sail for Canada, a still largely unknown country. Accompanying them on their adventure were their two sons, Wilfred Jr. and George, Wilfred's twenty-year-old wife Fanny (nee Osborne) and their first baby, Susannah. In a tragic turn of events, the infant fell sick as the ship approached Canada and died before they had even reached the wharf in Montreal. It was hardly the joyous arrival they had anticipated.

Following the baby's burial in Montreal, the group pushed on to Burlington, Ontario, where Wilfred Sr. and Susannah had prearranged to work at the Brant House, a "fashionable tourist resort and beautiful summer house." In many ways, this was a logical first step. In 1887 Burlington was a bustling waterfront community with strong ties to Britain and a busy tourist trade. The small town had a number of resorts, and

Wilfred and Susannah were well suited to hospitality work. The two boys took up commercial fishing, though they were hardly experienced, and together built a thirty-foot schooner which they named the *Lila*.

While the Frances remained in Burlington, awaiting their Canadian citizenship papers, they noticed an article in the *Toronto World* newspaper which wholeheartedly recommended the "unparalleled scenery, vastness and mystery of the channels and the islands around Muskoka Mills in northern Ontario." Intrigued by the prospect of yet another new challenge, the family decided to investigate the area.

I N THE SPRING OF 1890, WHILE THE REST STAYED BEHIND IN Burlington, Wilfred Jr. and George went ahead in the *Lila*, working their way through the Great Lakes system, up around Tobermory, then down the eastern coast of the peninsula, and across the Bay to Kaignashene, as it was then called. (The written record of Indian place names was never an exact science, hence the various spellings of Cognashene.) The two young men travelled by sail, with only the stars and their strong senses of direction to guide them. Wilfred's navigational prowess on this voyage earned him the lifelong moniker of "Captain Billy."

The brothers soon found work with the mills. In their spare time, the resourceful pair fashioned a shack for living quarters (using cast-off slabs) and a small cooperage factory at Shanty Point, a mile away from the mills. They did some fishing and outdoor guiding to supplement their incomes and in the winter months made barrels for storing and shipping fish.

FANNY'S PARENTS, THE OSBORNES (LEFT), FOR WHOM SHE AND WILFRED JR. NAMED THEIR HOTEL. AN EARLY CANADIAN PACIFIC PROMOTIONAL BROCHURE (RIGHT), QUITE POSSIBLY THE VERY ONE WHICH FIRST ATTRACTED THE FRANCES TO CANADA. FAMILY MEMBERS, INCLUDING YOUNG WILF (OPPOSITE, NEAR LEFT) AND FANNY (SECOND FROM RIGHT) GATHER AROUND THE DINING-ROOM TABLE TO STUDY AND READ. THE *LILA* (BELOW).

In the meantime, back in Burlington, Fanny was rearing her first son, Art. Shortly after giving birth in the fall of 1890 to her second, a boy named Clifford, Fanny and her new infant travelled to join Wilfred Jr. (Art, who was a toddler at the time, was left behind with his grandparents, who probably thought it wise to stay put until their prospects at Georgian Bay improved.) This must have been a difficult time for Fanny. Away from her young son Art, she passed a gruelling winter in a tiny cottage on the

WIND, WATER, ROCK AND SKY

FRANCEVILLE
AP 19
ONT.

A MINI-MUSEUM OF OLD FRANCEVILLE AND OSBORNE HOUSE ITEMS, INCLUDING A BOOT SCRAPE, THE ORIGINAL PHONE, FAMILY PHOTOS AND A TOOL BOX.

France Bros. Resort, Freddie Channel, Georgian Bay, Canada   Photo. by J. W. Bald

ed. This piecemeal approach was to become a Franceville trademark, and it accounted for the sometimes hodge-podge look of some of the buildings. From its humble beginnings as a boarding establishment, Franceville House eventually grew to include twenty-seven guest rooms, plus a boathouse with sleeping accommodations.

Franceville existed under squatters rights until the Crown began issuing deeds in 1915. At that point Wilfred "The Elder" acquired fifteen acres for $75 and Wilfred "The Younger," a somewhat smaller acreage for $37. The deed describes the combined property as being located at Brokenhead Reserve, concession #45, marked off by walking "astronomically north from the shore to the large pine tree, then bearing left, 20 degrees, and proceeding for 51 minutes to the western boundary, astronomically west."

F RANCEVILLE HOUSE FLOURISHED FOR THE FIRST TWENTY-five years growing steadily along with the tourist trade. In fact, the business was probably helped rather than hindered by the closing of Muskoka Mills in 1895, as it was after this time that tourists and early settlers began coming to Cognashene in earnest. Across the water on Minnicognashene Island, another hotel was up and running, though larger and very different in style. In contrast to it, Franceville was a family-run estab-

edge of the mill town, nursing her colicky baby.

It was two more years before the senior Frances joined their sons, by which point the family had formulated a plan. Though the mills were beginning to slow down, word of the area's abundant natural resources and spectacular scenery was beginning to spread. Hunting and fishing were powerful draws, attracting sportsmen and recreation-seekers first to the water's edge and then out to the uninhabited islands.

There was just one fly in the ointment: Not everyone in search of this wilderness experience actually wanted to camp. So here was an obvious and untapped business opportunity. The area's only guest house—the Rossin House—was tucked away in Muskoka Mills. In the spring of 1892, shortly after the senior Frances arrived at the Bay, the family began a lengthy building process that would last for years and end only after several buildings had been erected and expanded.

That spring, however, as work got under way, the Frances' plans were modest. One house for Wilfred Jr. and his growing family, another for Wilfred Sr., Susannah and George, with extra room to accommodate spillover millworkers and summer tourists—most of whom turned out to be American. Cognashene's first full-fledged hotel was beginning to take shape.

In typical France-like style, the family built an original, very basic structure—a well-proportioned building with a verandah extending in all directions visible from the water—and then added to it in stages, as money allowed and the market demand-

POSTCARDS OF FRANCEVILLE HOUSE (ABOVE LEFT) AND OSBORNE HOUSE (BELOW).

GUESTS ENJOY THE TENNIS COURT ON THE WEST LAWN OF OSBORNE HOUSE, 1920.

Unable to convince their father to slow down, and ready to build their own business, Captain Billy and Fanny began construction on their own hotel, the Osborne House in 1913. It opened for business the next year.

The new hotel was located just east of the Franceville House and the two businesses co-existed for four years. In October 1917, when Franceville House went up in flames, the edge of Osborne House caught fire, but it was saved by a well-organized bucket brigade. If there were any feelings of family resentment over the incident, or over the second generation's launching of a new and—there's no getting around it—competitive hotel, they didn't last for long. Franceville was entering a new era now, and it moved ahead in style.

The Osborne House was a grand hotel, larger and more elaborate than Franceville House. The main building resembled a four-layer wedding cake with a crow's nest perched on top and a second-floor balcony. The dining room sat forty-eight people, with additional guests accommodated at the family table

lishment—comfortable but not extravagant. Advertising was strictly word of mouth. Susannah and Wilfred Sr. shouldered most of the work—Susannah was an excellent cook—with the help of Fanny, and George and Captain Billy who hunted and fished and helped out in any way they could.

THINGS CONTINUED SMOOTHLY UNTIL THE FALL OF 1917, WHEN the hotel was destroyed by fire, possibly the result of mechanical failure. The northwest wind sweeping sparks down along the shoreline ignited the boathouse, too, which was full of boats stored for the winter and was consumed by flames in minutes.

Undaunted, Grandpa France—Wilf Sr., now aged seventy-seven—in poor health and losing his hearing, was determined to rebuild. And against the advice of everyone, he did, although the two-storey dwelling was never operated as a hotel as he had intended. It did, however, make a comfortable home for the senior Frances, who lived there together until Susannah passed away in the spring of 1919. Grandpa continued on alone in the house for another fifteen years.

This wasn't the first time the stubborn septuagenarian had dug in his heels. A few years earlier, Wilfred Sr. had refused Captain Billy's offer to take over the management of Franceville House. Retirement simply didn't suit Wilfred Sr., a man of immeasurable energy, even in his later years.

TOURISTS POSE ON THE PORCH OF THE ORIGINAL HOTEL.

GUESTS STAND IN FRONT OF FRANCEVILLE HOUSE WITH THE DAY'S IMPRESSIVE CATCH (ABOVE). THE FRANCE FAMILY CUTTING ICE IN 1908 (BELOW).

adjacent to the kitchen. There were several outbuildings, including stables, an icehouse, a planing mill, a chicken house, a cooperage, a machine shop, a smoke house, a root cellar, a family cottage, a windmill, a marine railway and a water tower.

The hotel also operated an official post office for guests and neighbouring cottagers. This was one of Captain Billy's many responsibilities, along with the tuckshop which was open during the mail sort. Fanny was a gracious hostess, who looked after the general welfare of their guests and saw to the running of the hotel

and the dining room. In the off-season, she dutifully corresponded with her guests. Fanny was also a meticulous bookkeeper as the accounts of the day reveal:

MR. PAUL BREITHAUPT	
2 PACKAGES CIGARETTES	.50
1 PACKAGE TOBACCO	.15
2 TINS MILK	.25
5 LB. SUGAR	.30
TOTAL (PAID IN FULL)	$1.20

Captain Billy's myriad talents included mechanics. He built the hotel's power

Last Visit to Franceville

IN THE LATE SIXTIES, A longtime Cognashener wandered through the deserted Osborne House, just prior to its destruction. Remembering the hotel in its heyday as he did, the experience was a nostalgic one for the cottager. He later recorded his impressions:

It was an eerie sensation to enter the darkness of the guest sitting room and the family living room. The baby grand piano was still there, along the west wall, the same one on which Fanny loved to play "Jesus Loves Me" with her thumb and forefinger. The remains of her wicker chair and Captain Billy's leather chair, where he played his flute in the evenings, were also there in the stillness of the family room. The old oak cabinet that had housed many books, the gifts of friends and guests, was there, and beside it the old wind-up phonograph. Old Maclean's magazines of the 1920s littered the floor along with letters for "Aunt Millie," or whomever, bearing short summertime messages hoping that the fishing, the picnicking and the swimming were fine.

OSBORNE HOUSE IN 1970, JUST A FEW YEARS BEFORE IT WAS LEVELLED.

Then up the creaking stairs holding onto the winding oak banister to the second floor and a peek into the master bedroom, Captain Billy's adjacent photo-developing room, and Wilf's childhood bedroom, just down the hall. And finally, with heart pumping now at a somewhat faster tempo, up the narrow, dark stairway to the fourth-floor crow's nest. What a view in all directions. It was here that Captain Billy liked to come each day in the few discretionary hours at his disposal. There was his work bench, the cupboard where the kites were kept and the homemade knitting machine which he enjoyed working on in the evenings. He would often knit late into the night and then retire to the kitchen for his ritual snack of canned lobster, crackers, old cheese and beer before bedtime.

I remember this last visit to Osborne House with a mixture of emotions. It was an exciting, somewhat frightening adventure, but rewarding for the memories it evoked of an irreplaceable old hotel.

THE ORIGINAL FRANCEVILLE HOTEL STAMP AND AN EARLY OSBORNE HOUSE BUSINESS CARD.

system—a Delco plant of wet batteries, which allowed for a single light-bulb in every bedroom. He also put in a telephone system connecting the four floors of the hotel and the surrounding buildings. Plumbing was fairly extensive for the times. Water was hand-pumped through pipes which drew from the Bay, and the outdoor "facilities" were referred to as "the Houses of Parliament," for they were indeed located up on a hill.

MAINTAINING DESIRED INVENTORIES OF ROOT BEER AND ALE for family and guests was an important undertaking shared by the family. "Making the Brew" merited special entries in the daily journal as phases of the maturing process were carefully monitored. It is also record-

ed that the late night sound of caps popping off bottles stored in the basement was not altogether uncommon.

Fanny planted an extensive vegetable garden each year, for practical reasons, and also a purple and gold dahlia garden which was her pride and joy. A section of lawn was cropped short and bordered with lime paint to serve as a grass tennis court for guests.

George—always affectionately known as "Uncle George"—was never an integral part of the hotel operation. He was a superb craftsman who built and repaired boats, and he also worked with neighbouring cottagers in the maintenance of their buildings.

Franceville was a busy place. Excursion boats frequently docked there

"The service was well attended and Dr. Reinholdt delivered a short and acceptable sermon."

and supply boats stopped by regularly with provisions. Cottagers came in the morning to drop off their laundry and their mail, along with their orders for groceries and hardware. They would return later in the day to collect their things when the Franceville boat returned from its daily trip to Penetang.

Socializing was a way of life at Franceville. All-day picnics were popular affairs and very elaborate in style—a location was carefully selected and laundry hampers filled with copious supplies of food and then loaded into the skiffs. Fishing was this early resort's predominant sport and the recorded catches of pike, bass, perch and muskellunge were impressive.

Community church services were frequently held at Franceville, on the large west verandah in good weather, and in the guest sitting room when it rained. For some in this makeshift cottage congregation, church had a strong social component. A diary entry on August 30, 1930 notes that, "The service was well attended and Dr. Reinholdt delivered a short and acceptable sermon."

NATIVE PEOPLE CAME AND WENT FROM Franceville, rowing or paddling the ten miles from Christian Island to sell their crafts, including the quill boxes with sweet-grass motifs still found in many cottages today. They often camped overnight when the weather closed in and were always welcomed by the Frances, prompting the Ojibwa to officially recognize

CHURCHGOERS ARRIVE AT THE BOATHOUSE (ABOVE). GEORGE'S DORY (BELOW).

"the kind acts of the France family in looking to our welfare in times of need."

At Christmastime in 1934, Wilfred Sr. died at his beloved Franceville at the age of ninety-five. In a dazzling display of Scottish stoicism, Fanny's journal entry on that day reads simply: "Grampa died at 1:30 this morning; put up six more curtains." Two years later, Captain Billy passed away at freeze-up time, too late in the season for a proper burial. The ice was poor that year, so he was laid out in the root cellar until he could be taken to Penetang in the following spring.

Despite these sad losses, life carried on at Osborne House until 1942 when guest invitations were discontinued. There was a shortage of supplies by this time and a dwindling roster of guests—cumulative effects of the Second World War. But there were other reasons, too. Fanny's health was failing and the proud older woman could no longer manage the physical demands of maintaining a guest house alone. After the business closed, she stayed on at the hotel until her

WILFRED SR. IN THE MID-1920S.

HEADING TO TOWN IN 1937, FROM LEFT: MR. CAMPBELL, CAPTAIN BILLY AND FANNY FRANCE, MRS. CAMPBELL, WILF, WINNIE, YOUNG JOAN AND GEORGE FRANCE.

death in 1958 at the ripe age of ninety-one, though by then the building was decaying around her.

And finally, the last of the first wave of Frances, dear old Uncle George, who had managed to sidestep the hotel business all those years, fell one night in the second-floor bathtub, sustaining a fatal blow to his head. It was 1960, he was ninety-five and virtually blind at the time.

Responsibility for the extensive Franceville property fell to Billy and Fanny's son, Wilfred III—commonly known as Wilf. It was an enormous task to maintain all the buildings, many of which were already in various stages of dilapidation.

The remains of the Osborne House were levelled in 1974, marking the end of a wonderful, though sometimes difficult, era. Wilf and his wife Winnie's home, and other restored and newly built summer houses, are now occupied by sixth-generation members of the family.

For some, passing by the shoreline evokes the memory of earlier days when Franceville was a hub of activity. Though there is little left now to indicate its unique place in the history of Cognashene, the original Franceville sign remains, anchored in the rock, firm and deep.

ONE HUNDRED YEARS AT THE HEART OF THE COMMUNITY

FOR THE LAST CENTURY MAXWELL ISLAND ON THE MAIN channel in Cognashene has been more popularly known as Whalen's, after one of the earliest, and evidently most enterprising, pioneers of Cognashene.

The history of the island as we know it dates back to about 1890 when it was the site of the bustling Muskoka Landing wharf, a dock designed to service the mills at the mouth of the Musquash River, three miles away. As the Muskoka Mills were difficult to reach, their operators built the wharf to provide steamer ships from Penetanguishene and Midland with a place to load and unload supplies and lumber. The docks remained in use until 1898, when the lumber industry moved out of the area for good.

They were still active when Elizabeth Whalen and her husband William discovered Maxwell Island. Residents of Penetanguishene, where William was an employee of the Breithaupt Tannery, the couple came in search of relief for Elizabeth's persistent respiratory ailments: asthma, allergies, and the like. In those days, conventional thinking imbued the bracing Georgian Bay air with all kinds of restorative powers, and regardless of whether this widely held theory had any medical validity or not, it seems it was a remedy for the fifty-year-old Elizabeth. With

GRANDMA WHALEN.

the permission of the Muskoka Mills management, she and her son, Charlie (one of eight children), began tenting on Maxwell Island in the mid-1890s.

Elizabeth was hooked on the Bay from the start, and after a few years of camping, desired a more permanent and comfortable arrangement. She negotiated the lease of the central part of the island with the mill owners and erected a small cottage. And so it was, in the late 1890s, that the spirited Elizabeth—or "Grandma Whalen," as she came to be called—became one of Cognashene's first and most illustrious summer residents.

When that first cottage burned to the ground within a year, Elizabeth simply had a new and larger one constructed on a different site. The new one suited Elizabeth even better than the first as she could now accommodate larger groups of friends from town. The fast-growing popularity of her private retreat obviously suggested a business opportunity to the magnanimous matriarch, because in the early 1900s (in time to catch the first wave of tourists), she constructed a small hotel and christened it the Whalen Island Summer Home.

Business was brisk from the start. As word of its hospitality spread, Whalen's Summer Home (its more familiar sobriquet) became a popular destination for a variety of guests, many of whom travelled from as far away as the United States. And naturally, several fell in love with the islands, bought land nearby and established their own footholds in Cognashene.

From the very beginning, the area's isolation created problems for the transportation of supplies, guests and the growing community of summer residents. In the earliest days of Whalen's, Elizabeth would arrive in the spring with a scow loaded with a cow, pigs, chickens and other essential supplies. And amazingly, her son Sam regularly rowed the twelve long miles from town in order to deliver provisions to the island.

O F COURSE, IT WASN'T LONG BEFORE OTHER EARLY COTTAGERS came to rely on the Whalens for their milk and groceries and someone—probably the energetic Elizabeth, once again—soon spotted another opportunity. A small supply "booth" was built on the waterfront in 1910 and manned by members of the family, including Elizabeth's son Charlie, until his death in 1912. That same year, Elizabeth purchased the entire island in order to expand the hotel. An icehouse was built and it became Sam's responsibility to travel out in the bleak midwinter to cut and store ice for both the hotel and summer cottagers.

With the advent of cottaging, steamships began to make daily trips up the Bay, departing from Midland and Penetang, bearing supplies, local pas-

WORKERS FROM THE BREITHAUPT TANNERY IN PENETANG, CIRCA 1890.

WIND, WATER, ROCK AND SKY

A FAMILY PHOTO CIRCA 1920
WITH MRS. WHALEN AT
THE BOTTOM OF THE STAIRS.

IN 1925 FIFTEEN-YEAR-OLD CHARLES
McGIBBON, BOB HALL AND OTHERS LAUNCHED
THE COGNASHENE REGATTA. THESE RIBBONS
AND CUPS DATE FROM THE FIRST DECADE OR
SO OF THE ANNUAL COMPETITION.

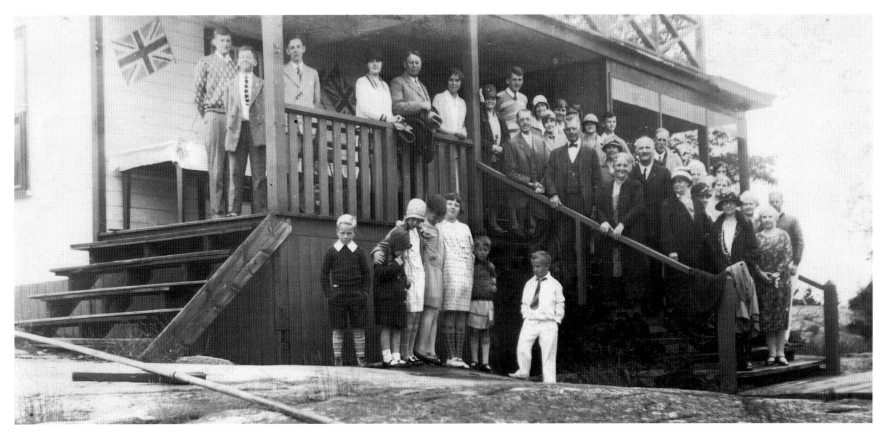

sengers and tourists. Among the many boats to land at Whalen's over the years were the *John Lee*, the *Waubic*, the *Midland City*, the *City of Dover* and later, the *Penetang Eighty-Eight*. What a thrill it was for cottagers of every age to watch these large and legendary vessels come and go through their waters, en route to Parry Sound and points north.

NO FLOURISHING SUMMER COMMUNITY WOULD BE COMPLETE without its very own post office, and Cognashene—even in those early cottaging years—was no different. Once again, it was the Whalens who took matters in hand, initiating Canada Post service to the islands. The first Whalen's Island Post Office was opened in June 1919, with Elizabeth's granddaughter, Lena (Gropp) Zoschke, acting as the first postmistress. This latest addition to the island enterprise served to cement Whalen's status as the heart and soul of the growing community. It also resulted in the daily gathering on Whalen's dock, known simply among Cognasheners as "meeting the boat." This afternoon ritual was to remain

a focal point of the day for decades to come, one fondly remembered by generations of cottagers for the opportunity it gave them to socialize and greet passengers, while they waited for their mail to be sorted.

Prospective guests and tourists were also made to feel at home—and in the centre of things—at Whalen's via a promotional brochure, circa 1920:

How to get to Whalen's Island—Should you plan your vacation by car, make Midland your headquarters, where there is ample garage accommodation; should the railroad be your mode of travel, the C.N.R. accommodates you, leaving Toronto 9 a.m. and arriving in Midland 1:35 p.m.; should you choose to make your trip via bus, the Gray Coach Lines have special summer service operating between Toronto and Midland and Penetang at least three times a day. The Georgian Bay Tourist Company of Midland operates the S.S. Midland City, giving excellent and convenient service to the 30,000 Islands, leaving Midland daily at 2 p.m. and arriving at Whalen's Island at 3:45 p.m. On Friday evening, at 7 p.m., a boat leaves Midland and arrives at Whalen's Island at 8 p.m., this service giving the city businessman the opportunity of enjoying a weekend at Whalen's Island, returning to Midland, via the Midland City, Sunday afternoon at 4:30. (All times are Standard Time.)

A store at the wharf supplies guests and surrounding cottages with all the incidentals of a drugstore, groceries, milk, ice-cream, vegetables, meats, gasoline, bait, etc.

Post office is on the wharf with daily boat and mail service in connection with the S.S. Midland City.

Basket lunches for fishing and picnic parties will be provided. Motorboats, rowboats and canoes can be rented for picnics, fishing, sunset and moonlight excursions.

Sunday services are held in the community by the Kaignashene Association.

During these years, Whalen's role as a binding force in the cottage community grew even stronger.

An annual regatta at Whalen's Dock is the highlight of the season.

Bracing Georgian Bay air at Whalen's is beneficial to sufferers from hay fever.

Whalen's Island is old in years and experience but young in hospitality and service.

Whalen's Island—where no one camps on your front lawn or monopolizes the bathing beach in front of your cottage.

Inevitably, this era of early growth and prosperity came to an end. In the fall of 1923, Elizabeth Whalen died, leaving her successful summer resort to her daughters, Rebecca (Whalen) Gropp and May (Whalen Adams) Manson. With the aid of other family members the sisters maintained both the hotel and waterfront businesses until late 1941.

During these years, Whalen's role as a binding force in the community grew even stronger. Early regattas were held at the main dock from 1925 until sometime in the forties when the water traffic off the island got to

A CROWD GATHERS IN ANTICIPATION OF THE *MIDLAND CITY*'S DAILY ARRIVAL IN THE LATE 1930S. THE *KEWANA* BELONGED TO JUDGE LEE.

be too heavy. And in the evenings after the regattas the cottagers would gather at the hotel for a party and awards ceremony. The hotel was also the obvious choice for community gatherings, including church services and meetings of the Cognashene Cottagers' Association.

The early forties were years of change for Whalen's. In the spring of 1941 May Manson died, and in the fall of the same year a major fire destroyed the big hotel. The previously enlarged annex and other buildings, including the waterfront business section, survived intact. However, in 1942 the island was divided into two parcels. Bill Manson, husband of the late May, took the vacant southerly parcel, and Rebecca Gropp retained the northern portion, which included the remaining buildings and waterfront business. The business area was then leased to John and Russell Cooper, two cottagers in the community.

A few years later, in the summer of 1944, Rebecca's son, Bruce Gropp, purchased the business area and central section of the island from his mother, marking the beginning of a new era at Whalen's. With Bruce at the helm, the annex of the old hotel was converted to a dining room and a number of new guest cabins were built. The tourist trade was reactivated and for the next few years Bruce and his wife Mina and family ran both the waterfront area and the hotel business.

WHEN BRUCE PASSED AWAY IN THE SPRING OF 1950, HIS SON Jack and daughter-in-law Marg came to Mina's assistance. After a year, the younger couple purchased the business and with their growing family attempted to maintain both operations. But in 1953, with the resort business dwindling, Jack and Marg decided to concentrate their efforts on the waterfront. A new "modern store" incorporating a new post office was built next to the old booth. Marine facilities were enlarged, a community radio phone was installed, and the Cognashene Supply Centre was born. At this time, the grand old dining room and guest cabins were reverted to family use.

Over the next fifteen years Whalen's thrived. Although the business primarily served the Cognashene area, boaters heading for other destinations were increasingly using the main inside channel, and stopping by Whalen's on their way. Many Go Home Bay cottagers became regular customers as their own community five miles up the Bay lacked such a store.

During the late 1950s and early 1960s the Junior Cognashene Cottagers

THE *MIDLAND CITY* PREPARES TO DOCK AT WHALEN'S (LEFT). A 1945 POST-CARD (OPPOSITE) SHOWS THE COMMERCIAL DEVELOPMENT OF THE PROPERTY.

WHALEN'S ISLAND RESORT

Invitation to Whalen's Summer Home

AN EARLY BROCHURE FOR THE Whalen Island Summer House modestly described the resort as follows:

The main house has a large airy living room finished in rustic style, a spacious dining room where for years a standard of excellence is maintained that ensures a quality of food unsurpassed by any hotel on Georgian Bay. A broad screened verandah overlooking the famous inside channel gives the effect of being on shipboard, with sail and motorboats passing to-and-fro.

The guest rooms are on the second floor, comfortable rooms each with a magnificent view of the Islands.

Among the many attractions at Whalen's are sketching, music, swimming, canoeing, sailing, photography, picnicking and fishing for fighting black bass, pike, pickerel and muskellunge within rowing distance of the Island.

The brochure description could easily have been written for a modern-day resort with one major exception: rates were quoted at $2.50 and $3 per day or $14 and $17.50 weekly—presumably including meals!

Association (JCCA)—a social and enterprising collective of teens—was particularly active, and the old dining room at Whalen's became a popular spot for their weekly dances. The biggest of them all—the "Regatta Romp"—was an annual event not to be missed on any account.

But the 1960s were also years of change in Cognashene. Cottagers were beginning to buy bigger and faster boats—and with them, acquiring greater independence. The taxi-boat business from Honey Harbour began to dwindle. At the same time, cottages were becoming better equipped with modern refrigeration. Daily trips to the local store were no longer a necessity.

With their children growing up and moving on, Jack and Marg Gropp decided in the summer of 1969 that it was time to close the family business for good and to enjoy the island in private with their family. It would be the first time in almost seventy years that there would be no business ventures on Whalen's.

In a letter written to the community late that summer their plans were announced:

Commencing September 2, 1969, all business facilities at Whalen's will be permanently closed, and all indications of commercial interest will be removed. It is our wish to assume a private identity as quickly as possible so that Whalen's can truly be our home away from home, completely divorced from business implication.

The *Georgian Tourist*, a local free press paper, ran a front-page piece on Whalen's that same month. A portion of the article read as follows:

A longtime friend to many a boatman, canoe-tripper and especially Georgian Bay cottager will close its doors for good when the summer holiday season is officially over after this coming weekend.

The Cognashene Supply Centre—simply known as Whalen's to its many customers among the lower 30,000 Islands—has evolved from a private summer retreat, to a small hotel, to a cottage resort, to a grocery store and marine gas station down through the seventy-odd years since it was first purchased by Mrs. [Elizabeth] Whalen of Penetanguishene.

Now it will revert to a private summer home for Mrs. Whalen's great grandson Jack Gropp and his family.

On this the twentieth anniversary of his taking over the summer business from his mother and father, Mr. Gropp decided this year to close up the store which he, his wife and children have run as a family team "and settle down to enjoy it a bit."

The family spent the following summer removing all indications of commercial interest. The old booth was torn down, the store cleared out, gas pumps and storage tanks ripped out. Docks were removed and all attempts were made to "normalize" the waterfront. Although passing motorists still came looking for the store, and the *Miss Midland* still announced Whalen's as a tourist attraction, life was quiet on the island.

The last twenty-eight years have seen myriad changes. Residential buildings have been removed, remodelled or new ones built so that the growing families can continue to share the island. Of the older buildings, presently only three of the cabins remain for the most part unchanged. The store has been expanded and converted to a waterfront cottage. The small cottage to the north of the old hotel is now the living room of a larger cottage. Whalen's has truly become a private summer retreat. A greater part of the island is owned and enjoyed by Elizabeth's great grandchildren—Jack Gropp, Helen Zoschke and Paul Zoschke—and their children and grandchildren, with some of the present generations enjoying Whalen's Island year round.

Some attempts at reliving the past have been made. The "Regatta Romp Revival" was resurrected during the 1980s. Once again as many as 200 cottagers and their friends drew together at Whalen's to romp, reminisce and, perhaps for some, to relive the summers of their youth.

What will the next one hundred years bring? It remains to be seen. For now, the island belongs to the descendants of Elizabeth Whalen. But for those who grew up in Cognashene prior to the seventies, summer and Whalen's will forever remain synonymous.

MINNICOGNASHENE

WHERE LITTLE BERRIES GROW

MINNICOGNASHENE IS PROBABLY BEST KNOWN FOR THE grand old hotel which graced its granite rocks for forty memorable years. But pre-twentieth century—in fact, long before white settlers discovered the island's abundant natural beauty—natives from the mainland paddled out to Minnicognashene in the summers to gather berries for their winter use, to dry their fish on the shores and generally enjoy a respite from the hungry mosquitoes.

The island's name is Ojibway and appears to mean either "the land where little berries grow," or "the land of many porcupines and berries," depending upon the translator, and perhaps even the spelling. The latter has varied during the last century, ranging from Minneacognashene, Minnecognashene, Minniacognashene and Minnecoganashene. Today, it is simply "Minnicog" to those who know and love it.

Did Champlain or his rascally young protegé, Etienne Brûlé, stop on her welcoming shores? It's impossible to say, but we do know that Minnicog's more recent history is linked to the founding of Penetanguishene. The British naval base established there in 1815, and the town that soon sprouted around it, attracted a steady stream of tradesmen, fur traders, immigrants and, of course, military personnel, all seeking to carve out a life along the developing shore of Georgian Bay. Among the latter was one Captain James Keating, adjutant of the military establishment and grand-

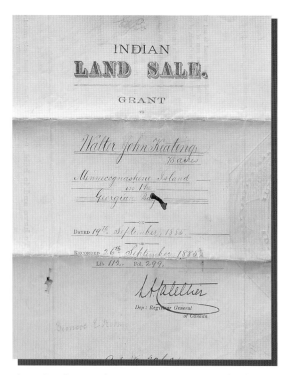

father of Minnicog's first owner, Walter John Keating of Penetang.

If little else is known about W. J. Keating, one thing is certain: When he purchased Minnicog, he made himself a deal. On September 19, 1885, he bought the seventy-five-acre island from the Department of Indian Affairs (the proceeds to benefit the Chippewa of Lakes Huron and Simcoe) for the princely sum of $75. Nobody knows for sure what his intentions for the island were, because just two months later Keating "flipped" the island for a handsome profit to Sir Roderick Cameron, an Englishman living in New York. The selling price this time: $350.

Though Cameron was probably responsible for the first small frame house on the island, situated in a protected bay on the east shore, he may have spent little time there during the next twelve seasons. In 1897, Cameron sold Minnicognashene to an American, William Woodnutt Griscom, for exactly the amount he had paid for it.

Griscom had bigger plans for Minnicog. He built the huge old house on the top of the hill which was to remain a local landmark for fifty-seven years. And to provide his children with a place to play, he enwrapped the house in a big broad verandah. (This was removed sometime in the 1930s.) Despite his interest in the island, Griscom enjoyed it only briefly. In a sad turn of events, he fatally shot himself on nearby Governor Island. A short time later, in 1901, his widow, Dora Griscom, sold Minnicog to Colonel John

Cumberland Cautley for $5,500.

At the time, Cautley had just returned to Canada from India where he had served in the British Indian Army. While crossing the Atlantic with his two sisters, Cautley made the acquaintance of a fellow named Billy Bushnell and hired him on the spot to be his "gentleman's gentleman." Cautley installed Bushnell and his wife Elsie on Minnicog, where the couple lived year round in what came to be called the Winter Cottage. Having undergone several additions and renovations, it still stands today, the only reminder of the Cautley era.

THE *WAUBIC* AT THE MINNICOG PIER, 1912 (ABOVE). THE ORIGINAL LAND DEED (OPPOSITE).

I T WAS SOON APPARENT THAT WHAT THE COLONEL REALLY HAD IN mind for the island was something in the way of a small business venture. Nothing too ambitious, just a quiet, out-of-the-way fishing camp. Cautley's idyllic sporting retreat was a hit from the start. As demand grew,

THE WINTER COTTAGE, CIRCA 1920.

Nothing too ambitious, just a quiet, out-of-the-way fishing camp.

THE DESCRIPTION ON THE
FRONT OF THIS POSTCARD
READS "THE MINNICOG,
GEORGIAN BAY."

he rapidly expanded the resort—too rapidly, it seems—and quickly found himself in financial trouble. In three years he had built twenty buildings, including sleeping accommodation for nearly 200 guests. If it sounds prosperous, consider this: Cautley's 1906 season was only six weeks long, while the minimum tenure for staff was three months. Something didn't add up. His profit that year was only $800.

TRAGEDY STRUCK AT THE HEART OF Minnicog again on January 5, 1908, when Colonel Cautley was killed by a streetcar in Buffalo. Through his will, drawn up only the day before, he left the island to his wife Lucy, with the Toronto General Trust as his trustee and executor. Lucy and their son, John, continued to enjoy the island for the next four years until they turned the management of the property over to Archibald Langmuir, an officer of the Toronto General Trust, and a trustee of the Cautley estate.

From 1912 until his death in 1938, Langmuir operated the hotel with the help of two managers: Captain Sam Malcolmson, and following his death in 1927, Arthur Russell, a resident of Penetanguishene. Russell and some of his six children ran the operation for the next ten years, which, despite the depression, were some of the hotel's busiest.

These were the salad days of Minnicog, the days of romance and carefree style when the hotel accommodated 250 guests. In addition to the many cottages, cabins and annexes, there were about fourteen tent platforms, reserved for the hardier outdoorsmen. The hotel's food was brought by boat from Penetang; the cooking catered to English tastes. One guest once recalled fondly that she had vacationed at Minnicog in 1912, and again in 1924. When she returned for a third visit in 1942, she happily ordered exactly the same Sunday lunch as she had had eighteen and thirty years earlier: roast beef *au jus*, pineapple sherbet and assorted cakes.

REGATTA DAY AT MINNICOG (ABOVE). A POSTCARD FEATURING A COLOURIZED J. W. BALD PHOTOGRAPH (BELOW).

The grand Minnicog pier in the east bay was visited daily by a string of steamers. The *Waubic*, *City of Dover*, and *Midland City* all conveyed passengers of the Grand Trunk Railway from Penetang out to the island for their Minnicog stay.

In the beginning, the large steamships docked on the north shore, where the old cribs can still be seen. Very few of Cognashene's rocky islands offer

ART RUSSELL AND HIS DOG, "MINNICOG MITCH."

any suitable surface for a horse and wagon, however, Minnicog's flat expanse of granite was *slightly* more hospitable. The guests enjoyed, or rather endured, their long ride in an iron-wheeled carriage over the rocks to the main house. The roadbed, made of clinkers from the steamboats' burner, covered the rough rocks, while the swamps were overlaid with "corduroy" logs. Baggage would be carried from the main pier in a horse-drawn cart, up the hill to the front door of the Green Cottage where it would be unloaded, unpacked and pressed by the hotel's housekeeping staff.

The guests enjoyed—or rather endured—their long ride in an iron-wheeled carriage over the rocks to the main house.

Outdoor pursuits were the primary focus of guests who were drawn to Minnicog at least partially for its plethora of such activities. It boasted a beautifully manicured bowling green and wooden-plank tennis courts. (The former was built by Colonel Cautley who imported several tons of soil for the purpose.) There was magnificent swimming on the eastern beaches and western rocky shores, and frequent fishing parties out to the open where the schools of fish were well-known to the aboriginal guides.

Boating and sailing were daily pleasures for the guests, as were formal picnics to neighbouring islands and blueberry picking—and eating! Just imagine the young ladies in their long, white cotton dresses being paddled through the islands by genteel young men dressed to the nines in white flannels and navy blazers. The same ladies "dressed" for the evenings, particularly when there was a dance, and the men occasionally donned dinner jackets and ties, though they reportedly preferred a more casual com-

THE HOTEL'S WOODEN-PLANK TENNIS COURTS (THIS PAGE). A 1908 J.W. BALD POSTCARD (OPPOSITE).

fort. (Pity the people saddled with Minnicog's mountains of laundry, not to mention the pressing. It's little wonder there were two staff for every guest in order to keep the operation sailing to everyone's satisfaction.) The social life on the island during the twenties and early thirties included local cottagers, enticed, no doubt, by the legendary parties and five-piece resident band.

How quickly things can change. Like so many other businesses the hotel failed to survive the Depression. Though some families continued to visit year after year, in the end they simply couldn't pay their bills. Beyond the hotel, this decline affected everyone in the area. Many of the neighbouring islanders had grown to love Minnicog and relied on it for entertainment and, more importantly, fresh supplies and mail. To make

matters worse, Archibald Langmuir passed away. When the hotel folded in the spring of 1938, Herbert C. Jarvis, a cottager from nearby Governor Island, stepped in. Together with his son, Bob, he facilitated the formation of Minnicog Limited and organized its financing through an $11,000 mortgage. This enabled the pair to take over the Minnicog property from the estate of John Cautley, which was still being managed by the Toronto General Trust.

Almost immediately, in June of that year, the Minnicog Yacht Club was formed to "operate a yacht, country and social club and to promote the welfare of its members." The club thrived for the next three years, serving the local community and visiting guests. It operated a hotel, post office and general store, and a summer program for the children of members and guests. Above all, it was a clever solution to the dilemma of

HAL FARNCOMB (LEFT) AND TREVOR MANNING UNLOADING SUPPLIES IN THE 1920S.

WIND, WATER, ROCK AND SKY

Boat Racing on Georgian Bay, Canada.

There were frequent fishing parties out to the open where the schools of fish were well-known to the aboriginal guides.

running a successful country hotel toward the end of the Depression.

On Minnicognashene, however, nothing stays the same for long. With the advent of the forties and the Second World War, Minnicog's fortunes shifted again. Most of the members of the yacht club joined the navy. Because of their experience on Georgian Bay, a good many of these men commissioned and sailed Fairmiles—small, fast submarine chasers ("Hornets for Hitler") which were built in Penetang, Midland and Honey Harbour—down to Halifax, where they operated in the St. Lawrence Gulf.

Life in general assumed a different complexion during these years. With many of the men overseas, families stopped summering at the Bay. Businesses suffered, not the least among them, the yacht club. In 1943, Herbert Jarvis responded to a proposal from Gordon Leitch, a club member and president of the Navy League of Canada. His suggestion to transfer Minnicog to the League was yet another creative solution to the island's financial challenges.

Happily, the Navy League put Minnicog to good use. It founded the

MANY OF J. W. BALD'S GEORGIAN BAY PHOTOGRAPHS, INCLUDING THIS ONE (TOP LEFT), WERE MADE INTO POPULAR POSTCARDS. (THIS PAGE) THE CATCH OF THE DAY, 1935.

Happily, the Navy League put Minnicog to good use. It founded the

Princess Alice Camp, a sailing school attended by hundreds of boys and young men. A great many stories have emerged from those years via the frequent visitors who come to revisit the land of their childhood fun and education. For instance, as penance for misdemeanours, cadets were made to scrub and sweep the rocks on the east bay to keep them pristine and clean from all forms of growth. (Luckily for both the lichen and the cottagers, it has returned in full beauty over the years, along with mosses, berry bushes, and pines.) The only remnant of the Navy League today is a cairn on the East Bay in memory of a cadet who lost his life at camp.

During the Navy League years and until 1956, the large family of Frank and Juanita Rourke lived on Minnicog year round—with Frank responsible for all maintenance. Life on the island made for an unusual childhood for the Rourke's six children, who learned to cope with both the elements and the sometimes painful isolation of being separated from their school chums across the frozen waters. An account of their unique experiences is recorded in Juanita Rourke's delightful book, *Up The Shore*.

IN 1951, THE GOVERNMENT TIGHTENED ITS REGULATIONS, REQUIRING military encampments to update themselves with steel structures and fire sprinkler systems. Given the all-wooden nature of Minnicog's buildings and the immense expense of meeting the new regulations, the Navy League chose to close the Princess Alice Camp.

In 1955, Minnicog turned yet another corner in its long and winding road. With the war over and the nature of cottaging changing, there was little demand for a yacht club. Under the terms of the Navy League arrangement, the Jarvis family had the first right of refusal for the island—under the same terms by which it was transferred to the Navy League in 1943. Margaret (Sidie) Jarvis, financed by her husband Bob, bought the

Princess Alice Camp, a sailing school attended by hundreds of boys.

island in May of that year, and Minnicog entered its current phase.

At the time that he and his wife took possession, Bob Jarvis counted twenty-five wooden-frame buildings—accommodation for 125 guests. Many of the structures, however, were in poor repair, unsafe even. In short order, Jarvis had most of the original buildings dismantled. The Green and Winter cottages, the tool house, pump house, stables, and the boathouse were left standing. Today, the Winter Cottage remains in use, the pump house is a bachelor residence for one of the Minnicog men, the tool house is an archival museum and the stables are rapidly disintegrating.

In 1956, Bob Jarvis hired Phil Robitaille to be the island's caretaker. Phil took up residence on the island with his wife Leola and their six children, and the family soon became an integral part of the Minnicog clan. In 1969, with its tiny population growing, the island officially became the property of the Minnicog Company of Jarvises. These days, it's beginning to resemble a hotel once again as new buildings are erected and expanding families pad the population. A typical summer weekend in the nineties sees some forty family members—descendants of Honey and Bob Jarvis, and their spouses, children and grandchildren—come to stay.

Minnicognashene Island has seen many changes in the last century. It has felt the swish of snowshoes and sleigh runners, the clip-clop of horses' hooves, the rumble and strain of cart wheels on rock, and the roar of the tractor. Canoes, steamboats, inboard and outboard launches, and sailing craft of every description have plied its waters. People have come and gone, buildings have been erected and razed. Trees have sprouted and grown strong, only to be blown over by the Bay's savage gales, or cut down or swept by fire. Only the granite remains unchanged, solid and enduring, with its millions of fissures, crevasses, valleys and concavities, a fitting inspiration for the spirit of Minnicog.

CHURCH ON THE ROCKS

GROUNDED FIRM
AND DEEP

WHEN CHAMPLAIN AND HIS VOYAGEURS TRAVELLED down the main channel of Georgian Bay en route to Huronia in 1615, it was in the company of four members of the Récollets, a branch of the Franciscan Brotherhood. Hymns and verse helped to while away the long hours of paddling, while evening prayers marked the close of every day. Organized religion had moved through—if not exactly *to*—Cognashene.

Only a few French missionaries actually lived among the Huron: the Récollets and, after 1626, the Jesuits, whose dream of a native Christian community went up in flames, quite literally, during the vicious Huron-Iroquois war of 1649. With their mission at Sainte Marie destroyed (and two of their brave brethren tortured and burned at the stake), the surviving Jesuits and some of their Huron followers, weakened by hunger and illness, turned on their heels and fled. Perhaps wisely, the Europeans stayed away from the area for the next hundred years.

By the second half of the eighteenth century, the British army was making inroads into Upper Canada, including the area around southern Georgian Bay, where they encountered another indigenous people, the Ojibwa. The military's progress and the mildly friendly reception of the area's native communities paved the way for the second wave of mission work. Throughout the nineteenth century, English-speaking Protestant

A CHURCH-BOUND REVEREND MATHESON.

and Catholic missionaries in Collingwood and Coldwater ministered to the native populations on Beausoleil Island and later on Christian Island, often accompanying their converts on canoe trips to Cognashene where they fished and picked blueberries.

Missionaries aside, the growing tide of European settlers naturally brought with it organized religion. As a number of lumber enterprises flourished around the southern end of the Bay, the demand for permanent churches rose.

From the time the village of Muskoka Mills was established on the Musquash River in 1853, Christian worship was an integral part of its community life.

The Muskoka Mills closed for good in 1898, just shortly before religion began to take root out on the islands of Cognashene, where the majority of first summer residents were clergymen. In 1900, Mr. Charles Cocking, a Methodist minister from Penetanguishene, bought forty acres of Crown land. The property stretched from the mouth of Kaignashene Lake, south around the point all the way to the bluff at the mouth of the Freddy Channel. Cocking and his family built two summer cottages at its northern extremity and soon began entertaining guests.

Not too long after the Cockings arrived, another minister, Reverend Thomas Bartley of Collingwood, discovered Cognashene while camping with his family. Eventually he, too, settled and built the unique cottage known as Blarney Castle, just after the turn of the century.

In the years that followed, the Cockings and Bartleys introduced others to the area, most of whom were also ministers—the Reverends Matheson,

Gilmour, Beattie, and Hagar, to name a few. Their longer-than-usual vacations afforded these men the time to organize a seasonal change in residence and to undertake the lengthy trip to Georgian Bay. Having decided to cottage in Cognashene, some bought parcels of land from the extensive Cocking holdings, and as a result, Methodist and Presbyterian clergy formed a nucleus of pioneer cottagers in the area. And naturally, it didn't take this group long to notice that something was missing in their new summer community.

THE COGNASHENE COMMUNITY CHURCH CELEBRATED ITS inaugural service at Blarney Castle in 1906, and for the next two decades Sunday services in July and August swung between the Cocking and Bartley cottages.

By the early thirties the congregation was growing and the worship services required more careful planning. The Cognashene Cottagers' Association formed a church committee (though the church was an independent body) comprised of three highly organized members: Ethel Butt, Edith Cooper and Harriet Sutton. Without a permanent church structure, the women selected various island locations—ones that had sizable cottages and extensive docks to accommodate large numbers of small boats. On Sunday mornings, boaters would tether their bow lines to dock rings, cast anchors out over the sterns, and put out bumpers to cushion neighbouring craft which moored alongside.

Fair-weather services were held on large open verandahs, while rain

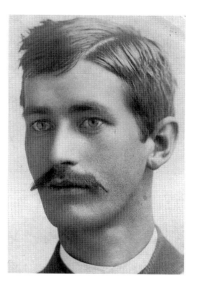

A YOUNG THOMAS BARTLEY.

forced the proceedings inside to large, cosy living rooms. Special-occasion services were hosted by one of the three community hotels: Franceville, Minnicognashene, or Whalen's, and from time to time services were also held on the Breithaupt's *Vancrofter* houseboat which was tugged out of Penetang for the purpose. The Breithaupt family diary entry on one such occasion reads: "We had a nice little service today. Dr. R's sermon was acceptable and not too long, this time. We all sang, I read, Mrs. Cocking said a nice little prayer and, on the whole, it was one of the best Sabbaths."

A POST- OR PRE-CHURCH GATHERING (CIRCA 1928) IN FRONT OF BLARNEY CASTLE, SITE OF MANY OF THE EARLIEST WORSHIP SERVICES.

The busy church committee also had the tiresome responsibility of arranging the weekly shunting of stacking chairs, the pump organ and the hymnals from island to island, and the dubious honour of selecting a vocal soloist and organist. Cookies and large quantities of lemonade were always on hand (courtesy of these same three ladies) to quench the collective post-service thirst and to allow an opportunity to mix and mingle since this was an event of some social importance. At the height of the "cottage era" of the community church—when services were held in various homes—twenty cottages participated.

Churchgoing attire has evolved over the years, though until the thirties it was typically formal. The women wore long white dresses with bows at the neckline and wide-brimmed straw hats. The men wore razor sharp grey flannels or white ducks, starched white shirts, dark ties and navy blazers. Naturally, everyone wore shoes and socks or stockings.

Without the distraction of a Sunday school, the restless children habitually slipped away after the collection hymn, disappearing into back rooms, verandahs and even down to boathouses where they would carry on out of sight. Some cottages were favourites—generally those with superior comic book collections. Others had a good supply of dolls or wooden boats. There were also rattlesnakes to tease in moments of boredom. Sequestered in these favourite spots, out of earshot of the sermon, the trick was to hear the last hymn in order to slip back surreptitiously just as the service wound down. Timing was everything.

Things eventually got a little more interesting for churchgoing teens.

DIVINE SERVICE

WILL BE HELD AT

AT 11.00 A.M.

Whalen Island – Mrs Brundgoff

Dr. Harold Hedley

July 16, 1950

A BEADED-LEATHER BIBLE
COVER FROM CHRISTIAN ISLAND
AND A WORSHIP SERVICE NOTICE
(THIS PAGE). A STACK OF SONG
AND PRAYER BOOKS (OPPOSITE).

There have been hymn selections usually designated for Advent, Christmas, Palm Sunday and Easter—all sung within a single service.

With the guidance of Reverend Vincent Bennett, a champion of Cognashene youth, the Junior Cognashene Cottagers' Association initiated Sunday evening singsongs in the late thirties. These were held in various cottages and even, on occasion, in boats tied to buoys in the channel. Everyone had their favourite hymn, though it was understood that "Will Your Anchor Hold in The Storms of Life" would be held for the finale.

Cognashene's church membership burgeoned in the the early fifties, as did the community's population in general. Weekly attendance in excess of 100 wasn't unusual. Docking accommodations became increasingly problematic and the faithful shuttlers of the stacking chairs, hymnals and the pump organ wearied of their weekly task. So in 1954, Louis Breithaupt, then lieutenant-governor of Ontario, and his wife Sara, gifted some property in the Freddy Channel as a permanent location for Sunday services. This was a turning point for what would henceforth be known locally as the "Church on the Rocks."

HAROLD HEDLEY, ISAAC CUTLER, AND ALAN BEATTIE, ALL OF whom were schoolteachers as well as sons of ministers, became lay preachers in Cognashene. They collaborated in the assembly of a six-by-eight-by-twelve-foot building as a storage facility, using cast-off wood from the dismantled Minnicognashene Hotel. Total cost of the project: $69. The building resembled a miniature church, even more so when decorated with the white cross and large bell donated by a neighbouring cottager.

Over the years a number of memorial bequests and gifts have gone toward such capital improvements as a dais, pulpit, communion table, electric organ, hymn books, loudspeakers, stone steps and railings, copious docking facilities, flower boxes, and a roof over the dais to shelter the minister and the organist in inclement weather. The unsheltered congregation knows to come prepared with raincoats and hats when the weather threatens. If rain is certain, services are held indoors at a cottage nearby.

In keeping with the times and the new location, there was a dramatic evolution of the dress code in the fifties and sixties to what is currently known as "Georgian Bay Wear." Apparel ranges from T-shirts, shorts, shredded sneakers and bare feet on warm days, to colourful parkas, toques and woollen mittens when it is cold. Social lingering is encouraged after church with the aid of lemonade and homemade cookies. This has become a welcome ritual, a bonafide "thirst after righteousness."

Just one of the many unique aspects of the church is its multidenominational makeup. Most summers see a variety of ministry styles come to Cognashene. Methodists, Presbyterians, Congregationalists, Unitarians, Episcopalians, Anglicans, United, Jesuit and lay persons have all taken part and assumed the lead in worship. And one never knows what's in store in terms of the order of service, texts, themes, and traditions on any particular Sunday. There have been celebrations of the Eucharist—the elements even being delivered to parishioners huddled in their boats on one rainy occasion. There have been hymn selections usually designated for Advent, Christmas, Palm Sunday and Easter, all incorporated within a single service. There have been reminiscences by ministers who grew up in the community, sitting among the assembly in their youth, and now addressing their family and friends for that first unnerving time. And of course there has been much said about God's gift of the rocks, trees, water, storms, sunsets and other natural wonders. For its part, the congregation has learned to be flexible

ONE OF THE FIRST SERVICES TO TAKE PLACE AT THE PERMANENT SITE OF THE CHURCH IN THE FREDDY CHANNEL BOASTED A FULL "HOUSE."

in the face of such pleasant idiosyncrasies.

And what of the ministers? Do Cognashene services require a different approach? Are they more challenging than a permanent charge? Few urban ministers need to contend with the weather to quite the same degree, or the distraction of black flies, mosquitoes, dragonflies and wasps. As anyone who's ever attended a service can attest, it isn't easy to swat—discreetly—while struggling to maintain your balance on a stacking chair, especially one that's wobbling precariously on the uneven rock. There may be a strong wind threatening to whisk away sermon notes and other liturgical accoutrements. And inevitably there are boats passing by in the channel, diverting attention, often at a crucial point in the service.

The Cognashene Community Church is no place for liturgical purists, it's true. The congregation—a mix of conservative and liberal styles—favours a blend of worship and nostalgia.

But there seems little doubt that for many Cognashene churchgoers these summer services are the most meaningful of all. For some, they're a welcome respite from the more routine worship of institutionalized churches back home. For most, they reflect a deep appreciation and love for Georgian Bay, and a pure delight at the opportunity to worship outdoors amidst the pines in the soft warmth of a summer day.

Of course, they have a point: There could be few places better than this, where, with just a little imagination, one can almost see eternity.

Cycles

BSERVANCE AND CELEBRATION of life's landmarks, notably those of a spiritual nature, are an integral part of the ethos of Cognashene.

Dora Halpenny so loves Georgian Bay that she arranged to be born on the kitchen table of her family's pioneer cottage on August 26, 1923. Her father, Dr. George Smith (a pediatrician, as luck would have it) and a colleague, Dr. Jim McCormack, were in attendance.

Wilfred "Captain Billy" France was so attached to his permanent home at Franceville that when he died at freeze up in 1936 he was laid out in the root cellar until the spring when he could be transported safely to Penetang for a proper burial.

Between the beginning and end of life, there are other events in which the Church on the Rocks has come to play a central role. Many a teenage romance has blossomed under the watchful eyes of a full moon, in a canoe gliding along the bewitching corridor of the Freddy Channel.

Ruth Cutler and Ed Cooper met in circumstances such as this, and their's was the first Cognashene marriage—a simple ceremony presided over by the principal of Emmanuel

THE FIRST CHURCH-ON-THE-ROCKS BAPTISM.

College at the Cooper cottage on Townsend Island, August 12, 1950.

The first wedding at the church took place on another August day almost twenty years later. The bride was delayed by buffeting winds and her father's reluctant boat engine, but eventually she arrived to the sound of heralding trumpets. Proceeding up the aisle—a slightly tipsy dock—the bride and her attendants advanced to the pink granite altar to join the groom who was flanked by his ring-bearing beagle, Daisy, and her own ring-bearing terrier, Rusty.

Ceremony completed, the newlyweds, Ann and Nicholas Elson, set out together in a brightly festooned, double-ended rowboat, the bride ensconced in a bower of flowers, relaxing in the stern, and the groom harnessed to the oars—with a flotilla of flowered punts trailing behind.

These celebrations made quite an impression and marriage "on the rocks" has become a popular community tradition. Since those initial nuptials, there have been eighteen weddings, and the church committee now requests that bookings be made a year in advance.

ED AND RUTH COOPER, 1950.

In step with the marriages, there have been eighteen christenings, five of which took place on a single Sunday. The first, on August 6, 1967, marked the baptism of young Kenneth Gordon Melhuish, who, the records show, was unusually well-behaved on this auspicious occasion.

While the observance of life's end has yet to become an official church affair in Cognashene, a number of urns are cached in folds of rocks beloved by the deceased, and there have been many sprinklings of ashes over the waters of the Bay. However, families of diehard Cognasheners planning such an exit in the future would do well to take note: In the evolution of this ritual cottagers have learned, through trial and painful error, that it's best to release the contents of their vessels on the leeward side of their boats on sunset funeral outings.

BLARNEY CASTLE

CHARACTER BUILDING

I
T's DIFFICULT TO IMAGINE TODAY BUT DURING THE NINETEENTH
century the majority of Canadians detested the wilderness. In the age
of the country's early development, it was seen as an impediment to
progress and a place of discomfort and hardship. General opinion began
to shift, however, as the railway moved across the country, connecting the
cities and towns with greater speed and efficiency.

By the turn of the century, the wilderness was assuming a whole new
appeal as a place of refuge and renewal. Urban areas were growing bigger,
dirtier and more dangerous, and many city dwellers—increasingly weary
of life in town—looked for relief to the forests and lakes nearby.

Such was the case for an intimate network of ministers—the clergy connection—who were some of the first to establish vacation retreats in Cognashene. Reverend Thomas Edwin Bartley, a native Irishman and
Methodist minister, was among their ranks. He and his family visited the
area in the late 1890s as guests of the Snetsinger family. With their friends,
they sailed out from Collingwood to camp, picnic and swim.

For the Bartleys, and others who quickly followed, the allure of the uninhabited islands was irresistible and land was easy to secure. The Bartleys
purchased their piece of paradise—a few acres around the curve of Cognashene Point—from the extensive holdings of Charles Cocking (the first
minister to arrive). The magnificent property, with its unfettered view

PHASE ONE OF BLARNEY CASTLE (ABOVE) AND A SLIGHTLY LATER VIEW (OPPOSITE).

which was rather modest—plain even, compared to the handsome landmark it would later become. Initially the family tented, while construction of a small cookhouse got under way. The main cottage was built shortly after in 1902 and connected to the kitchen by a breezeway—a disjointed design that was typical of the times. The idea was to protect early cottagers from undesirable cooking aromas and the contingency of the kitchen going up in flames.

Like so many old-timers, the boxy building sprouted new additions and decoration over the years, as time and finances allowed. (Jim Cooper, a great grandson of Thomas and Joed, and a current resident of Blarney Castle, observes that as a member of clergy, Reverend Bartley probably had plenty of the former during the summer months and somewhat less of the latter.) So Blarney Castle evolved over many years into a family centre full of comfort and character.

across the Bay to the western horizon, cost the family $40. At the same time, they negotiated with the government to buy the neighbouring Coney Island for $10.

Having purchased the perfect property, the Bartleys set about building the perfect cottage. In his work as a Methodist minister, Mr. Bartley enjoyed a reputation as a brilliant and energetic preacher, his gift for homiletics matched by his quirky sense of humour. His wife, Phebe Josephine—or "Joed" as she was called—was warm and capable. From its distinctive looks to its surely ironical name, Blarney Castle radiates the spirit of this pioneering couple.

Of course, none of this was evident in the cottage's early appearance,

Reverend Bartley was a keen and competent woodworker. He built three sturdy boats and handcarved a number of oars. The family's main boat, a wooden launch named the *Kathleen,* after one of their daughters, was built in their home on Gladstone Avenue in Toronto, and could only be extracted from its birthplace after an exterior wall of the house was removed. Much to Joed's delight, the wall was replaced with a greenhouse; an insatiable gardener, she could now indulge her passion year round.

Only Joed was permitted to operate *Kathleen,* a "one-lunger" with a distinctive putt putt that was recognizable long before she chugged into sight. (It was Kathleen—the daughter, not the boat—who later distinguished herself as one of the first female surgeons in Toronto, a founder of the Medical Arts Building at the University of Toronto, and

MEMBERS OF THE FAMILY RELAX IN FRONT OF THE JUST-COMPLETED COTTAGE IN THE EARLY 1900S (LEFT). A PORTRAIT OF THOMAS EDWIN BARTLEY IN THE EARLY 1890S (RIGHT).

WIND, WATER, ROCK AND SKY

A MODERN VIEW (OPPOSITE). A MID-TWENTIES COGNASHENE CHURCH CONGREGATION (ABOVE). JOED (BELOW LEFT) AND GUESTS ARRIVING IN 1930.

eventually chief of surgery at Women's College Hospital. In later years, she donated Cupid Island, opposite Cognashene point, for the erection of the Champlain Monument, a community landmark and tribute to one of the area's earliest visitors.)

The resourceful minister also built most of the cottage's furnishings including the icebox, dining-room table, cupboards, dressing tables and storage boxes for tools and preserves—all family gems which still occupy the cottage today.

IN 1902, MR. BARTLEY CONTRIBUTED $25 (FROM his annual salary of $1,100) toward the building of a large dock to serve the steamers and boats that frequented the area. Later, as president of the Kaig-

nashene Cottagers' Association (KCA, later the CCA), he provided sound leadership when the organization and four other island associations formed the Georgian Bay Association in 1916.

While her husband lent his leadership skills to early community efforts, Joed applied her own considerable ones at home. Turn-of-the-century cottaging in a place as remote and rustic as Cognashene demanded a certain fortitude, particularly on the part of the women, and Joed was well-suited to the life. Even after Thomas's death in 1919, Joed continued on at the cottage. She was undaunted by the prospect of long summers at the Bay, usually in the company of her sister Belle, her children, Tom, Kathleen and Gladys, and beginning in 1930, her two granddaughters, Lorna and

The newly washed items were rinsed in Bay water and draped over the juniper

(LEFT TO RIGHT) JOED AND MRS. GREEN CHOPPING WOOD; ISOBEL REINHOLDT (CENTRE) DRESSING UP; JOED (LEFT) AND A BEVY OF BATHING BEAUTIES.

Bernice. Similarly, she was untroubled by the long journey by car and steamer to get there—always by the twenty-fourth of May in order to get her gardens in on time.

These were Joed's pride and joy—the large vegetable beds behind the cottage and the extensive ornamental garden in front. Her lilacs, daylilies and tiger lilies were legends in her time and survive to this day, as do her sedum, mugho pine and carpathian walnut.

Capable, resourceful, highly organized—Joed was all of these things, and not surprisingly, a central figure in the growing community. It seemed only natural that Blarney Castle hosted many of the early church services in the days when cottagers converged by boat in their Sunday best, and gathered on the verandah, or on the rocks in front of the cottage.

In a similar fashion, the Bartleys and their visitors assembled weekly to do a large laundry in the boathouse under Joed's direction, with the aid of a hand-cranked washing machine and a rippling metal scrub board. The newly washed items were rinsed in cool, clear Bay water and draped over the juniper bushes to dry and whiten in a fashion ever so superior to that afforded by a clothesline. The juniper bushes imparted a wonderful fragrance to the freshly washed sheets and clothing so from May through September the Bartleys and their guests smelled perpetually "green."

It fell to the youngsters (Tom's two daughters) to fulfill a long list of chores, among them the unenviable task of running down to the old sawmill to collect rotting sawdust and horse droppings to nourish their grandmother's beloved garden. On the trip home, with the boat heavily-laden, the only place left to sit was on top of the manure pile!

Communal quilting bees, much chopping of ice and wood, popular "shore dinners" (picnics, by any other name), long, leisurely swims into the main channel, followed by long siestas in the swinging hammock: the days were a jumble of duties and delights. Despite much hard work, Joed kept her good humour, as was amply demonstrated the day she was photographed in the middle of the channel—standing on a shoal hidden beneath the water's surface—dressed to the hilt in dress, hat and parasol.

Her culinary skills were also a matter of record, though later in life, when her vision failed, her granddaughters were never sure whether the raisins in her legendary roly-poly pudding were really raisins or the pesky and ubiquitous "wood bugs." So the once famous dessert ended in ignominy when the children surreptitiously discarded their helpings in their laps.

Meal planning in general was a challenge for early cottagers, but Joed's system was a simple one: She hung a large slab of bacon in the screened-in verandah, to be scraped when the breakfast menu called for it. Klim, a

bushes to dry in a fashion ever so superior to that afforded by a clothesline.

(LEFT TO RIGHT) WILF FRANCE WITH THE LADIES; THE FAMOUS WALKING-ON-WATER INCIDENT; BERNICE BARTLEY PICNICKING WITH FRIENDS.

dehydrated milk product, was always on hand to be mixed with water and served as an important, albeit lumpy, staple beverage. (Wilf France delivered fresh milk from Franceville.) Joed made only occasional trips into Midland on the *Midland City*, and otherwise relied heavily on Preston's and Barry's supply boats which stopped regularly at a neighbourhood dock, loaded to the gunnels with provisions.

EVENINGS AT THE BARTLEY'S WERE ALWAYS EVENTFUL AND cosy, with the warmth of good friends gathering enhanced by the golden glow of the cottage's oil lamps. Card games (including the always popular "Flinch"), fully costumed charades and masquerades were favourite entertainments, only to be replaced by taffy pulls and popcorn making when the blinding squalls would come, setting the rain to dance its merriment on the rooftop. Bartley evenings always closed with bible readings and prayers before retirement to sleeping quarters on the open verandah.

On fine Saturday nights there were bonfires, music on the wind-up Victrola and the ritual reading of a favourite poem, "The Little Red Canoe." On calm Sunday nights small boats would raft together for community singsongs in the middle of the Bay.

Of course, all of this was many years ago. In 1975, the CBC stumbled on the charms of Blarney Castle and arranged to spend a week there filming a documentary called "*The Passionate Canadians—The Group of Seven, 1910–1920.*" The cottage's carefully preserved interior offered the producers a perfect snapshot of the era when, young and largely unknown, several of the Group of Seven spent time visiting and sketching in Cognashene. Ironically, they never actually set foot in Blarney Castle, but then even the CBC is entitled to its artistic licence.

Today, the cottage has been restored to its original splendour. Its gingerbread roof cropping has been realigned and renewed with fresh coats of black paint. The solid simplicity of the original building has been enhanced and enlarged by a longitudinal extension containing four new bedrooms, and there have been sundry other improvements.

The old icehouse, the corrugated laundry board, and the manure from the sawmill have given way to more efficient conveniences, but five generations after the Bartleys first arrived, certain family activities continue unchanged. The lily ponds are carefully perpetuated and the gardens fondly maintained. And family and guests still congregate to roast marshmallows and savour the Cognashene sunset as it dips into the horizon, seven leagues to the west, somewhere east of Lake Huron—and always, just this side of heaven.

AUNT EDNA   ALBERT KING

BILLY BRISSETTE   WILF

FRANCE   ORVILLE WRIGHT

CELESTE ROBITAILLE

LOCAL LEGENDS

AUNT EDNA   ALBERT KING

BILLY BRISSETTE   WILF

FRANCE   ORVILLE WRIGHT

CELESTE ROBITAILLE

AUNT EDNA   ALBERT KING

LOCAL LEGENDS

SHAPING THE CHARACTER OF COGNASHENE

Aunt Edna Breithaupt

MARTHA EDNA BREITHAUPT WAS ONE OF THOSE RARE PEOPLE, the kind so universally admired that even strangers affectionately called her "Aunt."

The creative and financial force behind Wakunda, Cognashene's unique—although short-lived—artists' colony, Edna could well afford to be generous, thanks to a successful family business. But if hers was a life of privilege, it was also one of profound action. Rather than just issuing cheques and retreating to the comfort of one of her well-appointed family homes, she devoted her life to one good work after another.

Edna was one of eight children whose father hailed from a long line of German leather tanners. At the time of Edna's birth in 1885, Louis Jacob Breithaupt was a man about the town of Berlin (now Kitchener), Ontario, operating a prosperous tannery and investing heavily in various other local business interests. He was also involved in civic, and eventually provincial, politics. In the same year that Edna was born, he expanded the family tannery, opening a second operation in Penetanguishene. A short time later, he established a family cottage there, too.

Edna's early life was a swirl of church activities, artistic pursuits, travel and summers at one of her family's two cottages (they maintained a second one at Riverbend, near Kitchener). After completing her initial studies at the Ontario Ladies College, Edna settled for a time in Toronto, where she immersed herself in the city's burgeoning art scene, filling her days with studio visits and instruction from the likes of Alex (A.Y.) Jackson. She also attended the Anglican Church, sang in a choir, and nurtured an interest in youth programs. (Though she would never marry or have children, education was to remain a lifelong passion of Edna's.) Fuelled by such earnest hobbies and a family history of charitable involvements, her strong sense of duty soon led her toward mission work in the developing world.

In 1920, by church arrangement, Edna was included as a delegate at the World Sunday School Convention on child welfare and education in

EDNA CIRCA 1915. (PREVIOUS PAGE) STUDENTS GATHER AT WAKUNDA IN THE EARLY THIRTIES.

Osaka, Japan. The following year, she returned again to the Far East to participate in a three-year famine relief effort in the China interior, south of Peking. Despite some truly harrowing experiences while travelling there (she seemed to delight in later recounting the tale of her trip up the Yangzte in the compa-

EDNA (ABOVE), SECOND FROM THE RIGHT.

ny of drunken sailors), Edna arrived in one piece and applied herself to this project with true missionary zeal. For her efforts she was rewarded with the gratitude of countless Chinese families and the affectionate prefix of "Aunt," which was to follow her for the rest of her life.

When she returned to Toronto, Edna refocused on her skills as a painter. She enrolled as a mature student at the Ontario College of Art (OCA) in 1926, where she received instruction from members of a newly formed col-

lective of artists who called themselves the Group of Seven. But like others around her during that heady time, Edna was something of a free spirit and she chafed under the institutional regimen of the OCA environment. Frustrated, she left the school at the end of her first year—along with a nucleus of other like-minded students—with the intention of devising a new educational model.

Full of ideas and confidence, this self-styled bohemian group embarked on a round of studio visits, studied the work of Canadian artists and received regular instruction from such future luminaries as Arthur Lismer and Alex Jackson. They also ruthlessly appraised each other's work in an effort to define a new approach to painting. Encouraged by the momentum that was gathering, Edna—who was, it seems, a born leader—formed the Art Students' League in 1927. Its official residence at the head of Grange Road incorporated the Grange Studios, Galleries and Craft Shop in a house rented from the Art Gallery of Ontario.

The *Yearbook of The Arts in Canada* was quick to praise the efforts of the fledgling group: "The experiment has already proved itself worthwhile.

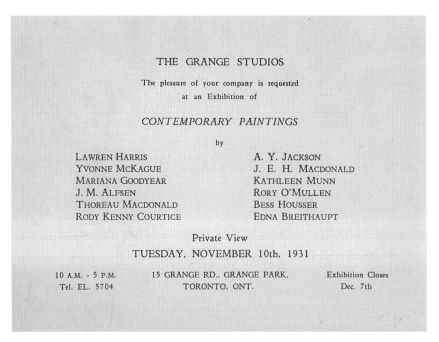

THE GRANGE STUDIOS

The pleasure of your company is requested at an Exhibition of

CONTEMPORARY PAINTINGS

by

LAWREN HARRIS	A. Y. JACKSON
YVONNE MCKAGUE	J. E. H. MACDONALD
MARIANA GOODYEAR	KATHLEEN MUNN
J. M. ALFSEN	RORY O'MULLEN
THOREAU MACDONALD	BESS HOUSSER
RODY KENNY COURTICE	EDNA BREITHAUPT

Private View
TUESDAY, NOVEMBER 10th, 1931

10 A.M. - 5 P.M.   15 GRANGE RD., GRANGE PARK,   Exhibition Closes
Tel. EL. 5704   TORONTO, ONT.   Dec. 7th

EDNA TRAVELLED TO CHINA IN THE EARLY TWENTIES, WHERE SHE VOLUNTEERED FOR A FAMINE RELIEF PROJECT.

Girls and boys of different races and different social environment work together, exchanging their ideas and holding life study classes and exhibitions. . . . Serious work has been accomplished."

The league had other admirers, too. Reviewing one of the group's 1929 exhibitions, Lawren Harris wrote in the *Canadian Forum*, "None of the work is stilted, none of it is blighted by academic dullness; almost none of its smacks of the schools. It is all alive in its own right, and vitally alive."

In its first year, the League had sixteen members, only two of whom were men. Sketching trips to scenic spots in southern Ontario dotted their agenda, including several excursions to the Riverbend and Penetang areas.

In the midst of this activity, Edna still found time to exercise her political interests. She involved herself in the National Council of Women, and may well have been the only woman on the executive committee of the Social Service Council. She also organized an exhibition of work by Canadian women artists, a show she eventually took on the road, where,

at a reception in New York, she caught the eye of the Lipton tea people. Edna was considered a minor Canadian celebrity by then, and as such was asked to do a testimonial on the spot. The endorsement read rather stiffly:

> *"I have travelled all over the world," said Miss Breithaupt. "Even in those countries from which fine teas come, I have tasted none that surpasses Lipton. I believe the brisk flavour, as you call it, is just right for Canadian women."*

IN SEARCH OF NEW LOCATIONS FOR HER ARTIST LEAGUE'S sketching classes, Edna was drawn again and again to the rugged beauty of Georgian Bay and, in particular, to Cognashene, where she had close family ties in the cottaging community. On one scouting trip in the late twenties, she discovered a cluster of islands in the Hang Dog Channel—the perfect location, she reasoned, for a seasonal artists' colony. She was most interested in six of the islands, and backed by family income she bought them all.

In the spring of 1929 Edna, now in her early forties, built a sizeable, though rustic, studio on Wakunda Island and circulated a pamphlet touting its scenic splendor and the potential for artistic advancement in a healthy, "out-of-door" setting. Furthermore, she advertised that it was for people of all classes, "not just the wealthy." No one can ever claim that

Its extensive programs now included painting, music, modelling, drama, writing, dancing, sculpture and crafts. Illustrative of Edna's holistic approach to life and art, she even engaged a "competent dietician to cater to individual needs," just for good measure.

Wakunda continued to flourish for a number of years, aided immeasurably by the involvement of various members of the Group of Seven. Ultimately, though, its success inspired its restless patron to even greater heights of ambition and idealism, both of which would be realized in her Wakunda National Community Centres of Canada, a series of facilities designed to expose Canadians to the wonders of the wilderness experience.

SOMETIME IN THE FORTIES, EDNA, RIGHT, A MINOR CANADIAN CELEBRITY, POSED FOR THIS LIPTON TEA AD.

With this scheme in mind, Edna purchased 600 acres at Saw Log Bay on the Penetanguishene peninsula in 1937 and built the Wakunda Lodge for students of the visual arts. Study sessions there were followed by exhibitions of their work in studios that Edna owned along a prime stretch of Bloor Street West in Toronto, which was also home to Wakunda's headquarters.

In 1947, by which point she was well into her sixties, Edna bought another large tract of land up the peninsula beyond Saw Log Bay, and over the water to include Giant's Tomb Island. This was no simple real estate investment. In keeping with the Wakunda vision, Edna's newest and grandest plan called for a fifty-acre estate for the advancement of the arts, to be located on Giant's

Edna's own financial comfort blinded her to the reality of others.

Wakunda, which in Ojibway means "The Universal God," was an unqualified success. But as with every other initiative of Edna's, nothing stood still for long. By 1934, just five years into its operation, a new brochure described an even broader mandate:

Wakunda Colony attracts tourists, artists, musicians, writers, naturalists, business & professional people, social and religious groups, industrialists, and family groups.

Tomb. She called this proposed artistic Utopia the Georgian Bay Estates.

The long process of development, typical of projects of this magnitude, lurched into gear with a full complement of planners, developers, architects and government officials. A 150-foot, steel-hulled luxury craft called the *Pathfinder* was purchased to ferry visitors to-and-fro and to allow close-up explorations of the island's craggy shorelines from the water. However, this was one dream of Edna's that would never come to fruition. With the project still in its planning phase, the health of its driving force began to flag, and in 1963 Edna passed away before construction was even begun. She was seventy-eight.

Though the project was permanently laid to rest, in some ways, Edna's wish for an accessible wilderness experience has been realized: Today Saw Log Bay is the site of many family cottages; Giant's Tomb is enjoyed by countless vacationers who cruise the Bay; and Wakunda Island in Cognashene, now formally known as Aunt Edna's Artists Island, is a cherished local treasure. There, on the northern granite outcroppings, families picnic, and swim in the pounding surf, not far from where a stone fireplace stands, the only physical remnant of the Wakunda studio. Close by, Edna's creative legacy lives on in "Art-on-the-Rocks," an annual community gathering and exhibition.

Though not as grand as her own plans for the Bay, Edna would surely be pleased by this. Clearly, the essence of her message lingers there still.

Billy Brissette

COGNASHENE IN THE 1930s WAS SO QUIET A PLACE THAT WHEN THE east wind blew you could hear the train whistle in Port McNichol, some eight miles away. It was almost as familiar a sound as Billy Brissette's "putt-putt" starting up as he began his ritual rounds to deliver ice or wood to the cottagers.

Little is known of Billy's life in Penetanguishene before he came to the area, another former city dweller in search of a Georgian Bay tonic. But whatever his malady, Cognashene was the cure. Billy thrived in the fresh air, building himself two cabins in a bay in Kaignashene Lake, one insulated and virtually windowless for the winter, another, little more than a shack, really, for summer, and settled in for several decades.

Physically, Billy appeared strong, though rather tall and slender. His uniform of high-top basketball sneakers and head-to-toe woollens was a familiar sight around the Bay. No one knows for sure if Billy actually slept in his signature hat, but suffice it to say, there are those who didn't recognize him without it. It was just part of his enigmatic charm.

Billy's residency was in the heyday of elegant wooden boats, and his

His uniform of high-top basketball sneakers and head-to-toe woollens was a familiar sight around the Bay.

small runabout with its beautiful wineglass stern and gleaming copper-domed engine cut a lovely figure on the water. Inside the boat was another story: water sloshed about beneath the floorboards, the result of melting ice and the inevitable leaks of a lapstrake wooden boat. Never one to miss an opportunity, however, Billy capitalized on this unique "feature," maintaining a stock of lively minnows in the bottom of the boat. With an old tea strainer at the ready to scoop them up, and his fishing rod always at hand, he could troll for his next meal on a moment's notice.

Billy was a bachelor with few family connections in Cognashene, though he was a close friend of Albert King. A bit of a loner, he always managed to keep himself busy. Though he had little formal education, he was a voracious reader. He regularly picked up his neighbour's *Star Weeklys* and *Cleveland Plain Dealers*, which he liked to trade for his *Police Gazettes*. This gesture caused one family some concern one year. Not usually readers of the *Police Gazettes*, the publication mysteriously turned up in the outhouse where a young grandchild discovered the world of axe murderers with it attendant buckets of blood and grew increasingly terrorized by anything that went bump in the night.

Newspapers weren't the only things Billy shared with his neighbours. Long before anyone realized they shouldn't be picked, he dispersed generous bouquets of wild orchids. Many a cottage table was decorated with bowls of water lilies gathered during his trolls through a weedy bay. Similarly, he was always generous with his gifts of blueberries, though he made it clear he wasn't averse to getting some of them back, baked in a pie.

Billy's delightful quirkiness extended to his business dealings. One of the area's chief ice suppliers, he called on cottagers several times a week to make deliveries. During these visits, he checked his customers' boxes carefully and if he figured there was sufficient ice left, he refused to deliver any fresh. More than one family learned, on seeing him approach, to stow their diminishing chunk under an overturned dishpan and return it to the box as his boat left for the next delivery. It was either that, or risk running out before his next visit.

YOUNG WILF FRANCE (OPPOSITE). THE WINDMILL HE BUILT AT THE AGE OF THIRTEEN (ABOVE).

Unofficially, Billy paid social calls several times a season. Before hydro had snaked its way up through the islands, most cottagers sat on their screened porches, bundled in the cool dark, talking away the evening. Billy, often arriving quietly on foot, would sit outside on the steps and suddenly, much to the surprise of the cottagers, inject himself into an ongoing conversation. Then, as a discussion would continue, someone might say, "And what do you think, Billy?" only to find he had disappeared into the night as silently as he had arrived. On very rare occasions he might bring his concertina and play some old French-Canadian folk tunes, the sort one might step dance to.

Sometime in the years following the Second World War, Billy suffered a paralysing stroke late one fall. The ice hadn't thickened up just yet, so Billy's old friend, Albert King, nursed him daily and tended to his household chores until he was able to transport him by horse-drawn sleigh to Penetang General Hospital. Eventually, frail and vulnerable, Billy was moved to a nursing home where, a short time later, he quietly slipped away, taking with him the gentlest days of Cognashene.

Wilf France

PEOPLE IN COGNASHENE LIKE TO TELL THIS STORY ABOUT WILF France. One day, he and his dog team hurried along the Freddy Channel over the thinning ice of early spring. His sledding technique—tried-and-true—was to maintain speed, never remaining in one spot long enough for the ice to give way beneath him. It was risky business, sledding in the shoulder seasons, but then Wilf was an inveterate risk-taker. Besides, he did it almost every day. Only *this* time, something was different. Maybe the dogs were slower than usual or the ice thinner. It's difficult to say, but as he skimmed along the narrows the surface heaved and then gave way beneath him, plunging Wilf into the icy water. After pushing the team back onto the ice, he swam around retrieving his supplies.

Later, in recounting the adventure, he could only shake his head, gen-

Wilf's enterprising nature made him indispensable in the community. Central to his activity was the delivery of passengers and provisions.

uinely disappointed he hadn't recovered a can of paint which had sunk to the bottom of the Bay. But then he never was one to bask in the glow of his accomplishments. Generous and unassuming, he always wondered what more he could have done.

Wilfred Archibald France was born in his parent's cottage in 1894, a third-generation member of one of Cognashene's first families. His parents, grandparents and uncle had settled in the Bay in the 1890s, where they built and ran the Franceville Hotel. His parents—Wilfred (Captain Billy) and Fanny—eventually established their own summer resort in 1914, the somewhat grander Osborne House, right next door.

Wilf was the fifth of Fanny and Captain Billy's six children and a natural at the practical things in life: hunting, fishing, bush work, boating, mechanics, carpentry and electricity. His conventional education was supplied courtesy of his mother, a former schoolteacher from Sheffield, England, who taught all of her children at home. He grew up to be a short, muscular young man, sturdy of body and mind, and well suited to the harsh reality of year-round Georgian Bay living. He was independent and resourceful, with a useful talent for invention and improvisation. And though he didn't know it as a youth, these skills would later come to bear in his working life.

In 1916, Wilf proudly went off to boot camp in Niagara with his two older brothers. But on the point of being shipped overseas he was issued an honorary, compassionate discharge, with an instruction to return to Cognashene to care for his aging grandparents. Never revealing his disappointment, he returned home and from that time forward made his family, the land, and the various businesses they operated his priorities.

It was still some years before Wilf had the good fortune to meet the young and adventurous Winnie Lewis, a frequent visitor to a cottage in north Cognashene. During the first couple of years of their courtship, Wilf

taught the city-bred Winnie to hunt, fish, and to generally fend for herself in the bush; clearly he was grooming her for life in the wild. They were married in 1933 and enjoyed a long and loving partnership, punctuated by the birth of their four daughters and marked by years of hard work.

Wilf's enterprising nature made him just as indispensable in the cottage community as he was around Franceville. He built docks, boathouses and cottages, wired them, and installed Delco plants. He cut ice in the winter and exhibited a particular talent for mechanical work.

Central to his business activity was the family freight and delivery service. There were five France boats which Wilf used over the years, the most memorable of which was the fifty-foot, carvel-built *Sagamo 2*. It had an oak superstructure, a powerful Kermath engine and a wheelhouse cabin forward. It could go anywhere, in any weather—and Wilf tested its limits several times, venturing out when others wouldn't have dared. And while his passengers may have felt nervous, they always knew they were in capable hands: Wilf had an unerring sense of his vessel's—and his own—limits. His crossings of the gap between Penetang and Minnicog, often during raging storms, are the stuff of local legend, as cottager Arthur Jennings once recalled:

There was a gale blowing. We wouldn't risk going out in our boat and Granny wouldn't have let us even if we had wanted to, but with Wilf it was all right, so we joined him on his regular route. After rounding the buoy off Pinery Point, Wilf placed the range lights in line and, turning Sagamo hard over, steered a course true north toward The Gap.

Dusk was coming on as we negotiated our way around a large log boom heading south. We had a full load of passengers, groceries, lumber—everything you could think of was aboard that boat. The waves were enormous. The women and children were seated forward in a dry place; we sat atop a

WILF FLIES ACROSS THE ICE ON THE "GO-DEVIL," HIS HOMEMADE PRECURSOR TO THE SNOWMOBILE.

pile of lumber in the stern. We stalled in the middle of The Gap and thought out loud that with anyone else but Wilf we would be scared pink. In fact, we felt as safe as with our mothers in church. Our intrepid captain took his time as he pulled the carburetor apart, reassembled it and put us on our way just in time to clear the bank of shoals off the Gin Rocks.

With the rain pelting down, Wilf straightened his cap with purpose, flicked the longest ash I've ever seen from the end of the cigarette permanently in the centre of his mouth, and squinting through the bleary windshield, re-established his bearings and carried on, threading his way through the mischievous current in Gendron's channel and thus to the safety of the Freddy Channel.

OF COURSE, WITH WILF, EVEN SOME-
thing as innocuous as his daily runs into Penetang for mail, laundry and supplies, inspires

WILF'S PREFERRED MODE OF SUMMER TRAVEL.

stories of folkloric proportions. In the days when cottagers relied on him for deliveries and chores in town, they would converge on Franceville each morning, shopping lists in hand, though they knew not to arrive too early. Wilf, who habitually stayed up most of the night tinkering with motors and other gadgets, was always a bit of a late starter. Fortunately, the shopkeepers on the other end understood his idiosyncratic schedule and kept their doors open until he arrived. It wasn't unusual for Wilf to return from his rounds sometime after midnight.

Winter was a whole other challenge for full-time residents like the Frances. During these months, Wilf was often the only link to the outside world. (Remember, these were the pre-telephone days.) He would still regularly go to town, but just to be on the safe side Winnie would record the exact time—"1:23 p.m. on a sunny, cloudless day"—that he disappeared around the point. He didn't always make it home the same day, but Wilf had a unique arrangement with a Toronto radio station. On the nights when he didn't arrive back, Winnie knew to tune in to the 11 o'clock news on CFRB and await the coded message, usually to the effect that the ice around the point wasn't good and the party in question was staying in town for the night.

The water was flowing at the time of Wilf's last trip to town, one dark June night in 1970. Wilf was seventy-six at the time and his job that day was to deliver a telephone and refrigerator out to the islands. The first sign of trouble came when he lifted the fridge from his boat at Waubec Island and felt a sudden, unfamiliar pang of pain. When someone remarked that he didn't look well, Wilf insisted he was fine and carried on to deliver the telephone. He arrived home at 1 a.m. clinging to life, but satisfied that the day's deliveries were complete. He even managed a few lighthearted remarks about his condition as he was helped from his boat and up to the cottage for the last time.

In typical France family style, the next day's diary entry simply recorded that, "We are all so sad, for Wilf has died today and we will miss him." It was a sentiment shared by all who knew him well.

Albert King

NOBODY KNEW COGNASHENE LIKE ALBERT KING.

Born in 1892 at Gloucester Pool, Ontario, to parents of French extraction, Albert spent his entire life either on or near the water. While his father Sigefroid Roi worked as a foreman at various lumber camps

ALBERT'S FIRST CABIN, 1930S.

around the Bay, and his mother Corine as a camp cook, young Albert and his nine brothers and sisters grew up playing around the mills and along the shores of the rivers that powered them. (Curiously, many family members—Albert among them—would later change their name from Roi to King in an effort to assimilate with the area's predominantly British settlers.)

Eventually, Sigefroid moved his large family to Penetan-

(ABOVE) ALBERT'S DAUGHTERS, BERNICE, RITA, AND MARGARET AND BERNICE'S DAUGHTER ANNE, IN PENETANG.

guishene, where young Albert became reacquainted with his cousin, Leah Cadat, whom he married in July, 1913. A half-hearted attempt at farming in Tiny Township (named, incidentally, for one of three lapdogs belonging to the wife of John Graves Simcoe) followed their wedding, but the settled life didn't suit the peripatetic Albert, and his discontent was only compounded by the fact that he was no longer near his beloved water.

So it was back to the Bay for Albert, where, for the first thirteen years of his marriage, he held a series of logging, guiding or fishing related jobs—including the post of game warden on Beausoleil Island. Albert was in his element during these years. Meanwhile, Leah stayed at their permanent home in Penetang, where she bore the trauma of an astonishing ten miscarriages. It was seven years into their marriage before the couple had the first of their three daughters.

In the spring of 1927, Albert, by then thirty-five and the father of two girls, rowed quietly into the uninhabited Kaignashene Lake. He landed his boat near a flat point of rock beside a long stretch of earth, one of the few in the beautiful but desolate landscape. From this vantage point he could see clearly down and all around the lake. He'd found exactly what he was looking for; Albert had come to Cognashene to stay.

In his first years there—in fact, for the first twenty-five—Albert simply squatted on the land, a common practice in those days. He erected a one-man/one-dog lean-to the first season (to accommodate his faithful canine

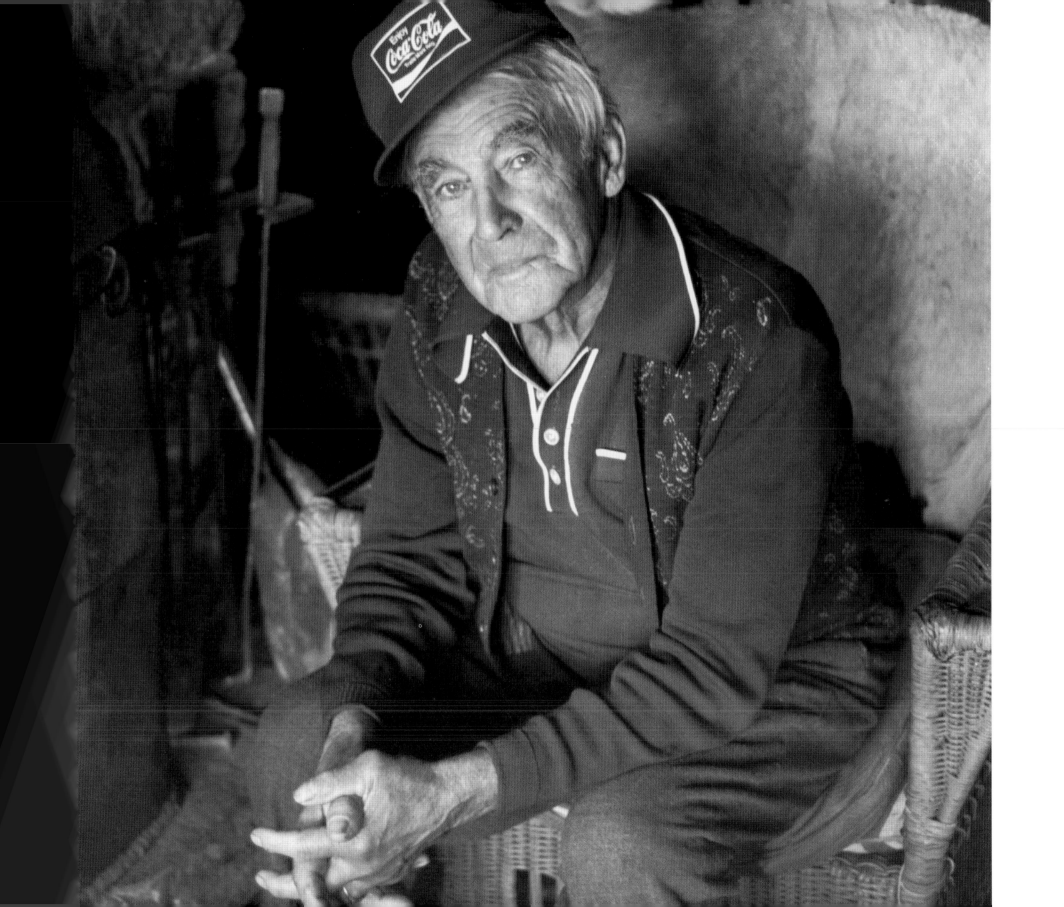

sidekick, Ti-Pitt), while he cleared the land and gathered the materials to build himself a simple cabin. When it was finished, the one-and-a-half room cottage was a recycler's dream come true: sunken slabs from the Musquash River—souvenirs from the mill days—formed the walls, while lumber, wooden shingles, and cast-off windows were salvaged here and there, and birch bark insulated the home. It still stands today, a testament to his building skills. Throughout the 1930s, Albert cultivated his small piece of paradise, while Leah and the girls continued to live in town.

Albert was carving out a life for himself in the tiny community of main-

ALBERT'S MAIN CABIN ON COGNASHENE LAKE IN THE LATE FIFTIES.

ALBERT'S MAIN CABIN ON COGNASHENE LAKE IN THE LATE FIFTIES.

ly French heritage settlers that inhabited the shores of Kaignashene Lake. He made a comfortable living hunting, fishing and trapping, at first, but before very long he hooked up with another year-round resident, Billy Brissette. Together, they "put up" ice in the winter and delivered it to cottagers in the summer. And more importantly, the two men, who lived two bays apart, forged a firm and lasting friendship.

Albert also planted an extensive potato garden and sold his produce as far south as Honey Harbour (ten cents for a seventy-pound bag), along with wood for $2 a cord. He established a small barnyard, populated with pigs, horses, sheep, cows and geese, and between 1938 and 1940, enlisted the help of his son-in-law, Celestin Dupuis, in the construction of a permanent cabin.

Of course, it wasn't long before summer cottagers began to look to the

kindly and capable Albert for help with a variety of projects, a reliance which eventually blossomed into his appointment as association caretaker. He was a quick study who could master just about any task, which made him awfully handy among the islands, but he had a remarkable natural ability when it came to gardening and landscaping. Evidence of his green thumb still flourishes all over Cognashene.

"Pepère was the greatest teacher in the world," muses his granddaughter, Nancy (Swales) Pilon. "He would warn you in the morning to stay out of the garden if he heard a rattler for he knew where it was. He could show you all the different herbs in the bush, or where the fishing might be good on any given day, or he could take you up the Musquash and give you the greatest history lesson about the lumbering days.

"There is a saying in French Canadian that, 'The smile is mainly from the eyes.' Oh, how Père's beautiful blues could talk."

WHILE ALBERT FORGED A LIFE AND LIVING AS A GENERAL BUILDER, labourer and stonemason, Leah and their three daughters—Bernice, Rita and Margaret—visited frequently, pitching in with the opening and closing of cottages (a regular responsibility for Albert) and helping out with occasional light housekeeping. It was his season-end chores for the cottagers that earned Albert his reputation as a bit of a tippler. It seems that without fail, Albert would go missing at least once every season during his closing-up rounds, only to be discovered late at night by his worried friends, propped up in someone or other's living room having refreshed himself a little too enthusiastically from the cottage's liquor stores. No one ever seemed to mind though; it was always considered part of his charm.

While Leah made an effort to fit in for a while, even baking delicious breads, pies and tarts for the always receptive cottagers, her interest in Cognashene lasted only as long as the warmest weather. At the first sign of fall, she retreated back to town. It was a unique arrangement, to be sure, though their marriage and affection for each other never seemed to suffer from it. Albert was devastated when Leah passed away in Penetang following a heart attack in the mid-1960s.

In 1967, Albert retired as the association caretaker to focus on his home and artistic endeavours. Occasional odd jobs aside, he devoted his remaining fifteen years to the leisurely pursuit of his hobbies. He continued to perfect his idiosyncratic surroundings in pragmatic ways—nurturing his flower and vegetable gardens and fixing up his four cabins—and on weekends he generally stood by, waiting with a twinkle in his eye to receive the

CELESTE ROBITAILLE WITH HIS SISTER LILY AND HIS COUSIN, STELLA KING JUNEAU.

boatloads of family and friends who came calling.

When Albert King died in the early eighties it seemed to those who knew him like the end of an era—one that spanned the years of the lumber trade, early settlement and tourism, and the more recent decades of modern cottaging. In all that time, Albert knew exactly where he belonged—in Cognashene where his influence outlives him still.

Celeste Robitaille

CELESTE ROBITAILLE WAS TWENTY WHEN HE CAME TO COGNASHENE in 1932, and in his own unassuming way, he changed it forever.

Drawn to Kaignashene Lake by family ties and his search for work, Celeste could hardly have known then what Cognashene would come to mean to him. But it did seem from the start that he was well suited to life as a year-rounder: He was a cheerful, resourceful young man with an enor-

mous range of talent. Shortly after arriving from Cedar Point on the mainland and moving in with his uncle Henry King, he found work cutting and supplying ice, a business he inherited from Billy Brissette, who in his advancing years had begun to find the work too taxing.

Typically, Celeste has many fond memories of this laborious task:

One of the first things I did was to build a big icehouse. It was made of poplar logs and had a roof of pine limbs and juniper. I got the sawdust from up the Musquash. The icehouse was thirty-by-fifty feet and we would put 2,000 blocks of ice in it every winter. It sounds like a lot, but I worried every summer that I wouldn't have enough to last the season, especially when it was hot. In the winter, we would wait until the ice got really thick. Sometimes it got to be about thirty inches deep. We usually cut in the little narrows by Jack Burke's place. We'd take our big saws and start cutting in a square. We did it all by hand. We used a saw that was ten feet long; I still have it. The saw had to go all the way down to the bottom of the ice. We'd cut in a straight row, then crossways, and make the block by using a chisel. Some of those pieces weighed as much as 300 pounds and we'd lift them out with big tongs. Then we'd cut the ice into blocks about sixteen-by-twenty-four inches and line them all up like bricks for a house. Every block had to go in the icehouse the way it came out of the Bay, so they'd all fit.

We'd use teams of horses, too, to help with the hauling and once in a while a horse would just disappear through the ice. When that happened, we'd rush up and get the stays off to let him loose and then we'd pull on the line to help him get out. In all my life we only lost three—and with all the horses we used that's not many. The horses often kept us out of trouble. No two days would be the same because the current would eat away at the ice from underneath

and though it looked safe on the surface, you could go through when you were least expecting it. Some of them just knew when the ice was dangerous and would shy away from the rotten places.

One time we had a horse cutting ice down at Kirby's island and he was afraid of the water. We couldn't even get him down to the water's edge to drink. Then after lunch one day, he was acting strange. All of sudden he took off right across the ice toward the open, and then went straight down about fifty feet. We got him out as soon as we could, but by that time he was frozen to death. The way that horse bolted, it was as if he wanted to commit suicide and knew what he was doing.

It was really hard going getting that ice out, but I was glad to have the work.

C ELESTE MOVED OVER TO HIS UNCLE ALBERT KING'S CABIN IN 1934, about the same time he launched a string of micro-businesses, working at times with his brother Phil. This was the beginning of Celeste's general contracting business, which catered to the growing cottage community and in those years earned him twenty-five cents an hour. Mechanics, carpentry, plumbing, stonemasonry, cottage and dock building—it seemed there wasn't anything this jack-of-many-trades couldn't do.

But then Celeste was never one to rely on just one source of livelihood, and besides, even in those early years of cottaging, when there was much building and expanding activity in the summer community, forging a living was a difficult challenge for the full-time residents. An enterprising attitude never went astray. Celeste always had at least one sideline on the go, and it was trapping in the early years. He maintained up to 150 lines for muskrat and mink, which he monitored by paddling down to the Musquash and back by the Shadow River, or travelling over the ice in winter. On a good day, he would catch as many as twenty, skin them on the spot to minimize the weight and, if he was lucky, sell them for seventy-five cents a pelt.

During the prohibition years, Celeste managed another small business, though his production of moonshine was more of an avocation, really. Using stainless steel kettles out behind his Uncle Henry's house, he boiled water, brown sugar and Fleishman's yeast with prunes or raisins to produce a substance which he then steamed through curly pipes. The residue was filtered through gravel and charcoal, and the end result— never more than forty proof—was a crystal-clear liquid which he coloured and flavoured to create gin, rye or rum. Having a personal supply certainly came in handy when he and his friends were feeling festive, but by and large he distilled it with an eye to selling it for $3.50 a gallon. Never a dull moment with Celeste around.

Life settled down somewhat after 1936, when the twenty-four-year-old married Leona Leroux, a teenager from nearby Perkinsfield. It was tough at first for the young couple, who tented and then built a small log cabin on a squat in Kaignashene Lake. (The family later purchased the property and continues to live there today.) These were lean years. With little money coming in they relied heavily on Celeste's hunting activities and homegrown vegetables to help put food on the table. Celeste can even recall a time when they ate nothing but fish for three weeks solid—three meals a day, seven days a week. And he chuckles when he reflects that they

learned to cook it in every way imaginable.

Fortunately, as their young family began to grow, so did Celeste's business prospects. While he continued to ply his various trades, Leona, always quiet and unfailingly kind, kept the books, a complicated and thankless task if ever there was one. Years later, in 1965, when the couple finally engaged a professional accountant, it was brought to Celeste's attention that he should think about paying some income tax!

In the late-forties and early fifties, Celeste twice tried his hand at lumbering. The first time was in partnership with Jack Burke, an Englishman of modest means living in Penetang; the second time, under the patronage of Senator Leighton McCarthy, who hoped to revive the family mill at the mouth of the Musquash River. Both businesses looked promising early on, but failed—through no fault of Celeste's—before too long.

In the meantime, Celeste turned his attention to his own pet project, that of establishing a school for the local children who lived in a cluster around Kaignashene Lake. He petitioned the cottagers for their support, and despite significant opposition, managed to sway the cottagers' association and solicit the assistance of the Minister of Education, who arranged for the project's financing. A property was acquired in "the Kaig"—the local reference to the lake—and a building was moved to the location and equipped, blackboards and all, from an abandoned school in Perkinsfield. Celeste

was made a Trustee and devoted a good deal of his time and energy to ensuring that his own seven children (four boys and three girls) received the formal education he had never had. At its high point, the single-room schoolhouse, which operated during the summer months only, accommodated twenty-nine students. When the local children outgrew the school, the little red building was sold and converted into a summer cottage.

But the school was only one of the ways in which Celeste made his mark. Sometime in the early sixties, he began wrestling with a way to broaden the passage through the Kaignashene Narrows in order to allow his work boats and barges to pass through from the lake into the Bay. Before he could take any action, Celeste needed the approval of the federal government. Happily, a local cottager, a Minister of the Crown at the time, paved the way, and with the help of thirty-five barrels of dynamite, Celeste was able to widen the narrows.

In 1970, at the age of almost sixty, Celeste embarked on yet another new career. These were the post-Whalen's days and Celeste was keenly aware of a hole in the local retail market. So he purchased a central piece of property in the Freddy Channel for the purpose of opening a store. For four years his waterfront operation provided local cottagers with fresh produce and meat, and gas for their boats, and tourists with a place to stay. Leona's sister Blanche was engaged to manage the business, while Celeste made daily trips to Penetang for supplies, and continued to oversee his various other work crews.

Sadly, Leona fell ill in 1974, prompting Celeste to sell the store (which

CELESTE AT WORK AT HIS SAWMILL AT THE MUSQUASH RIVER IN 1952 (TOP LEFT).

HIS SUPPLY STORE, GAS STATION AND MOTEL IN THE FREDDY CHANNEL (BELOW).

still operates today as Wanderer's Cove) so that he could spend more time at home. After a brave struggle with cancer, Leona passed away.

Celeste would continue to work for some years following Leona's death, alongside their sons who were assuming more responsibility in the family trades, but even the hard-working Celeste eventually warmed to the idea of retirement. Remarriage in 1980 to Dorothy Emes (a former CBC employee from Toronto), regular trips to the family's vacation retreat near Sudbury, and a steady stream of social engagements have filled Celeste's later days. And so, he claims, have his fond memories of the many people who've touched his life, and the times—good and bad—that have shaped his gentle spirit.

Cognashene is indeed lucky that Celeste Robitaille came looking for work: It is a far richer place for his presence.

Orville Wright

IN THE END, THE CHARACTER OF EVERY CENTURY IS MEASURED by its greatest advances. Telecommunications, cars, computers, the Net— it would be fair to say that few inventions in the twentieth century have had the impact of the flying machine, a spectacular event made even more romantic for the fact that it was the brainchild of two unassuming young brothers—Orville and Wilbur Wright, partners in a Dayton, Ohio-based bicycle business. Against all odds, and in the face of strong French competition, the Wrights logged the world's first official flight at Kitty Hawk, North Carolina, on a cold December day in 1903. It was one of this century's greatest leaps in scientific achievement.

It was years later, in 1916, that the middle-aged Orville Wright came to Cognashene, in search of a little peace and quiet. It was certainly a low point in the great aviator's life. He was suffering from sciatica—a painful back ailment exacerbated by an 1908 plane crash—and besieged by legal problems. Perhaps worst of all, Orville was still in lingering low spirits over the sudden death of his brother Wilbur from typhoid in 1912.

On the recommendation of a family friend, Orville agreed to a vacation in Cognashene where he stayed at Waubec Island in a cottage that belonged to the Williams family of Kitchener. The holiday was a tonic for Orville. Away from the pressures of work and publicity, he immersed himself in cottage life.

Esther Williams, the twenty-year-old daughter of Orville's hosts (and no relation to the Hollywood swim queen), toured him around in her outboard that summer, showing him the sights and introducing him to the pleasures of Georgian Bay picnics. It was on one such outing that Orville first noticed Lambert Island, his attention drawn by the eerie banging of shutters and doors against its abandoned buildings, and by the strong prevailing winds driving waves up the vertical rise to the west.

Orville was easily seduced by the drama of both Lambert and the Bay (perhaps the wild wind and waves reminded him of the Outer Banks of North Carolina). He bought the island soon after his return to Dayton that fall, and though he failed to visit the following summer, he came again in 1918 to initiate extensive renovations. When the construction was finally completed, his complex incorporated a main cottage, the appropriately named cliff house, a guest house, pump house, icehouse, outhouse, boathouse, a water tower and a funicular railroad.

It seems that even Orville may have underestimated the force of a good Georgian Bay blow. He confidently perched his cliff house on the edge of a promontory where it was exposed to the full force of the wind, though it was secured to the rocks with cables. At least it was until the day Orville noticed that the cabin had shifted off its foundations. Sitting down with a pencil and paper, he calculated that it would take winds exceeding 100 m.p.h. to move the building. Still astonished, he had it dismantled and moved to a less vulnerable location.

Orville's quirky island retreat boasted a number of innovations. The 300-gallon water tower was powered by a pump and gasoline engine. The odd little railroad/lift was operated by a reconditioned outboard motor and used to transport ice, provisions, baggage and guests from dockside to cliff top; in addition to its practical applications, it had great entertainment value. As did the fact that Orville refused to hang any curtains—anywhere—holding firmly to the notion that drapes were for people with something to hide, though many of his guests begged to differ.

THE FATHER OF FLIGHT WAS A LIFELONG STUDENT OF MANY subjects, in particular, astronomy. In order to indulge his interest he had the roofline of the main cottage lifted and a second storey added and furnished with comfortable lounge chairs and a powerful set of binoculars, as well as instruments to record the vicissitudes of the wind. From this perch, he had an unobstructed, 360-degree view of the heavens. He also spent endless hours in the cliff house, sixty feet above water level, which afforded a magnificent view of Minnicognashene, with its hotel, and beyond to Giant's Tomb and Hope Islands.

Orville and his sister Katharine spent many happy years together on Lambert. Close all their lives, Katharine had played an integral role in the race to take flight, offering encouragement and support in any way she could. At a pivotal point in her brothers' progress, she and Orville had even struck an odd bargain, promising to eschew marriage—at least until the boys were well and truly launched—in order to devote all their energies to the project at hand. Katharine upheld her end of the agreement, but years later, when she chose to marry a Kansas City journalist—after their invention took flight—Orville still considered it a betrayal. He never forgave her, and the once warm relationship was all but severed.

Though intensely private at times, Orville could also be sociable and was a gracious host and charming visitor. He entertained a variety of people at Lambert, including Griffith Brewer, the British balloonist, and Vilhjalmar Stefanson, an Arctic explorer. A steady flow of family came and went and invariably Orville, slim and wiry all his life, would meet them at the dock in his conventional cottage garb: a dark blue business suit with cuffless trousers, stiff white shirt, shiny oxfords and spotted bow tie. Scipio, his faithful St. Bernard, was often at his side.

Orville, a bachelor all his life, was a capable cook, self-taught in the kitchens of his aviation camps. Breakfast was his favourite meal; he was especially fond of toast, though his predilection for extra-thick slabs required him to design his own toaster. The end result accommodated three-quarter-inch slices, which, naturally, he had to slice in his homemade slicer. He preferred his toast dry, hard, racked in the Scottish

ORVILLE (LEFT) AND GRIFFITH BREWER.

tradition and smeared with butter and his own tart, orange marmalade.

While not much of a fisherman himself, Orville was always happy to indulge his guests when they presented him with catches of pike and smallmouth bass, which he panfried and served accompanied by his famous hollandaise sauce. Seldom were meals complete without a special Lambert Island blueberry pie.

Not surprisingly, Orville had a passion for boats and engines and in the twenty-five years that he vacationed in Cognashene he had a variety of watercraft. However, his greatest pride was the long, sleek launch which he acquired from Gidley in 1931. When Orville wondered what to call the

magnificent thirty-two footer, his pal Alex Jackson suggested "Kitty Hawk." Initially, the modest Orville shunned the idea, but A.Y. wasn't easily dissuaded. The artist connived with Carrie, Wright's faithful housekeeper, to arrange the letters as a Christmas present. In spite of himself, Orville was touched by the gift and had the shiny chrome letters shipped to the marina at Gidley. The next summer he arrived to find them installed, erroneously, as they now read: KITTYHAWK.

Ironically, he was never able to tune the boat's original engine to his liking. After ten years of tinkering, he finally gave up and purchased a powerful new Kermath engine from his good friend Wilf France, who combined his own mechanical skill with that of Orville's in its installation.

ONE OF ORVILLE'S GREATEST CHARMS WAS his wry sense of humour, which he delighted in turning upon himself, as he did on one memorable occasion. Having taught himself to sail—in a manner of speaking—he set out for dinner one evening in his fourteen-foot Ackroyd. With his hosts' welcoming bonfire as his beacon, he sailed before the wind. But when the principle of tacking momentarily escaped him, he headed straight onto the rocky shore and on up into the bushes. With dignity intact, he stepped from his boat and with a twinkle in his eye announced to the startled gathering his pleasure at having just been appointed an "honourary member of the Minnicog Yacht Club."

Orville's Cognashene days ended suddenly in 1941. In midsummer of that year the U.S. Army sent an envoy to Cognashene requesting his return to America where his advice was needed on aeronautical matters, and where it was deemed his security could be better managed. America was on the brink of joining the Second World War. Orville never returned to Cognashene. His health deteriorated throughout the forties and he died in 1948 at the age of seventy-seven.

In 1952, Wilf France bought the *Kittyhawk* from the Wright family. In the sixties, its hull was punctured at dockside when it broke loose from its moorings during a violent storm. Wilf suspended it in slings to protect it

THE SLEEK KITTYHAWK IN THE MID-THIRTIES, WITH ORVILLE AT THE WHEEL.

from water rot and later moved it ashore where it remained for some time, weathering and decaying over the years. The buildings on Lambert, once more abandoned, also began to deteriorate.

IT WAS TWENTY YEARS BEFORE THE *KITTYHAWK* SAW ANY ATTENTION. In 1972, Wilf's daughter Katherine bought the boat for her husband (Guy Johnstone) from her father's estate, and together they determined to restore it. Considered by some to be beyond repair, the launch was coaxed back into mint condition.

Complete with its reconstituted Kermath, a gleaming mahogany hull,

burnished breastplate and a replica of Carrie's original lettering, the splendid *Kittyhawk* was rechristened on June 29, 1975, by Orville's niece who travelled from Dayton to Midland for the occasion.

Completing the route that Orville had travelled so often, his prized launch proceeded with escort to Lambert, now three owners and much refurbishment later.

There, the relentless winds that the gentle man loved so well continue to buffet the granite cliffs, high above the water where he spent countless hours gazing out over the horizon, savouring the solitude and contemplating the future of flying machines.

WHEN WE WERE YOUNG

~ POWER AND GLORY

WHEN WE WERE YOUNG

POWER AND GLORY ~

REFLECTIONS

WHEN WE WERE YOUNG

~ POWER AND GLORY

WHEN WE WERE YOUNG

POWER AND GLORY ~

WHEN WE WERE YOUNG

WHEN WE WERE YOUNG

VOICES FROM THE PAST AND PRESENT

I N MANY WAYS, COTTAGE LIFE HAS CHANGED VERY LITTLE IN
the hundred years since the first settlers arrived. Oh, we get there
faster now, it's true. And once there, we experience few of the hard-
ships, the daily grind of difficult chores, that those early pioneers
endured. But picnics are still picnics, socials are still socials—or rather,
parties—and kids will always be kids. The ageless allure of the wind,
water, rock and sky still works its magic on every generation passing a
carefree summer at the cottage.

It's not so surprising, then, when tales are traded—generation to generation—that the pastimes of today's young cottagers are remarkably similar to
the youthful adventures of their parents, and even their parent's parents.
Variations on a theme, perhaps, but fundamentally the same old shenanigans.

Swimming, blueberrying, bonfires, overnight canoe trips—is it any wonder these popular pursuits have withstood the ravages of time and fashion?
Or that on a rainy day, gathering in the kitchen to make popcorn, play
cards, puzzle over jigsaws or generally indulge in lazy Georgian Bay hobbies, is still one of the finest ways to pass the time?

We came to appreciate at an early age that whatever the season held for
us there would be fun, adventure and good friends with whom to share it all.

If the following reveries prove anything at all, it's how fortunate we were
to spend our youthful days in Cognashene.

CAMPING OUT IN 1931 AND DRESSING UP IN 1926 (RIGHT): TWO TIMELESS ACTIVITIES THAT HAVE CAPTIVATED GENERATIONS OF YOUNG COTTAGERS.

Several Slices of Cognashene Life
The 1920s: Ruth Wilson

GEORGIAN BAY WAS THE FOCAL point of our lives when we were young. I still remember what a long journey it was to get there. The leaves on the trees would just be coming out in May during our springtime departure. We took the train from Brampton to Midland and invariably would have to wait for the mail from Toronto before the steamer set out for Whalen's Landing "up the shore." The steamer's arrival was the social event of the day and smaller boats would converge from all

CHARLES MCGIBBON AND A GOOD DAY'S CATCH, 1924.

about to pick up their passengers and take them to their islands.

The men had only a short twenty-four hours on the weekend before they would have to catch the steamer back to the landing on Sundays. Mother was left to cope with her brood of seven children all summer long with only primitive means of doing the daily chores. Wash day involved soaping the clothes in a copper tub with a paddle we worked by hand, and scrubbing the tough spots out on those wooden boards with their rippling

CRUISING THE BAY IN 1932 (ABOVE) WITH GOOD FRIENDS AND A FAST BOAT. MUGGING FOR THE CAMERA IN 1933 (BELOW).

metal surfaces. We'd hang everything out to dry on miles of clothesline and I remember how wonderfully fresh everything smelled, flapping in the breeze.

Mother did all the cooking over a woodstove and in the heat of July the temperature in the kitchen was unbearable. She also somehow managed to have everything done by Friday to be ready for the weekend. What a mixture of aromas and how good it all smelled. Weekends were eventful, with all our activities taking place on our twelve-acre island. We blueberried, and we played tennis—always in whites, of course—on the wooden courts Daddy built. We picnicked and had a rollicking good time in the

thundering waves that crashed along our northern shore. Daddy had built a pagoda, which still stands to this day. He would sit there in his blue kimono and think, and tut-tut at the children when they ventured too far out in the water.

Charades were a highlight on Saturday night. We must have accumulated enough costumes to clothe a small theatre company. Sunday unfolded in true Methodist fashion. Mother would greet us early, and after a breakfast of porridge and muffins we would gather around the piano for singsongs that lasted all day. Mother had delicate little fingers that would trip tirelessly across the keys. Mostly we sang hymns, but by arrangement guests would bring

MEMBERS OF THE SMITH, HORWOOD, AYER, MAHAFFY AND ALISON FAMILIES (ABOVE). CHILDHOOD FUN AND GAMES (OPPOSITE).

sheet music from modern musicals and Mother, who clearly expressed her disfavour over these choices, only played them out of courtesy. That piano is still in use in our cottage and it brings back many happy memories.

They were simple pleasures, back then, but we had great fun.

The 1930s: Bernice and John Cooper

IT WAS IN OUR MID-TEENS THAT WE FORMED the JCCA. I remember distinctly the major incentive for doing so was that there were two obnoxious young Tom Sawyer types (in the view of we older ones) with whom we preferred not to asso-

CHARADES IN THE 1920S.

ciate. They were thirteen, so we set the entrance age at fifteen. Our association meetings were serious and we took detailed minutes. We wanted to buy property for a clubhouse, but our parents wouldn't hear of it.

Our serious business centred around organizing picnics, collecting wood for Saturday night bonfires and preparing for Sunday night singsongs. We always did pantomimes at the bonfires. Two people would hold up a large white bedsheet and someone would stand behind the actors, usually two or three of them, and shine a flashlight to silhouette the action. The budding thespians would spring out from around a corner and plunge a dagger into the hearts of the oncomers. The theme was always the same, but we still

161

squealed with delight every time the dagger sunk in.

There were no telephones then, of course. We didn't even have modern radios. But some of us had crystal sets and it was a thrill to settle under the eiderdown at night, pull the covers over our eyes and listen to "The Shadow" in the dark, with the wind whistling through the pines. In retrospect, our pleasures then seem simple and repetitive, but we had wonderful times.

1940s: Duggan Melhuish

WE HAD A CLUB, AND AMONG OUR INITIATION RITES WAS SMOKING butcher string wrapped in toilet paper. It made for a hot smoke and our papers, rather like a diaper, became soggy quickly. Nevertheless it seemed a very important, macho thing to do at the time. We also caught snakes

Our serious business centred around organizing picnics, collecting wood for Saturday night bonfires and preparing for Sunday night singsongs.

and skinned them for making belts. We were particularly keen on rattlers and fox snakes because of their bright colours and diamond-patterned skins. We'd slit them down the underbelly and place the entrails on a breadboard to test the old tale of the heart beating until sundown, and discovered there was some truth to this belief. We oiled the skins for pliability, wrapped them around leather thongs and sewed them tight. We were very proud of our belts—designer fashion before its time.

The *Midland City* featured a special shopping day each Thursday and we always looked forward to "going to town." We would play the slot machines on the second deck and Billy would play the piano. When we got to town we headed straight to our favourite record store to play 78s until it was time to catch the boat home. On the trip back we would

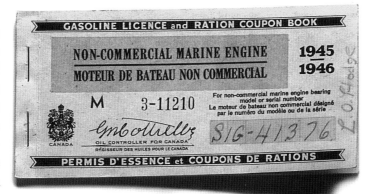

throw bread crumbs to the seagulls that circled and swooped and they would catch them in midair. The ship's smoke-stack belched filthy black soot and we couldn't wait to get home for a swim.

On Saturdays, the boys would chop down dead pine trees, haul them in old wooden dinghies to vacant islands of choice and stack them in the fashion of a pyramid. Our Saturday night group would gather after sundown and when we lit our pyramid it would spring to life with a tremendous whoosh, spitting sparks in all directions. As I walk those many bonfire islands today, the scars of the hot fires that cracked the surface rock are still visible. The mere sight of them inspires fond memories of the things we did on those glorious summer evenings.

And the games we played around the fire when it rained and squalled. Happy Families was special among those whose parents were of British origin. Bloody Stump, Snap, Fish, Ramoli, Monopoly—but the best of all was Hearts. Northern Cognasheners with a 1940s training in Hearts are the Minnesota Fats of the game. When it comes down to the wire

NEVER TOO YOUNG TO START PULLING HIS WEIGHT, DUGGAN MELHUISH HELPS HIS FATHER IVAN IN 1935.

THE IDEAL PLACE FOR AN AFTERNOON PICNIC.

they just never lose.

It was great to be young in the forties.

The 1950s: Valerie Wilson

DURING THIS TIME THE JCCA HAD THE LARGEST membership of its existence. It was fully organized with annual dues and elections for president, secretary and treasurer. Records were kept of members and events and new members were actively solicited. All activities were announced with wonderfully artistic posters made by Keith Hilmer and posted at Whalen's. We were most independent, acting without any parental supervision, although Marg Gropp was famous for her curfew enforcement.

Every Sunday night was Singsong, held at a different cottage. Someone played the organ and we sang hymns—our favourite, of course, was "Will Your Anchor Hold"; we always sang it last. Bonfires were held at the Lizard, picnics at Aunt Edna's, and weekly dances in the old dining room at Whalen's. We all loved music and we especially loved to dance. The old floor really moved. Regatta Romp at Whalen's was the highlight of the summer. The hall was always decorated for the dance and as many as fifty people might come.

"Girls-only" events centred around pyjama parties, the most notorious of which were held at the Genge's. Once, we played strip poker and the entire group had to run around outside the cottage after every strip; another time, seven girls snuck out in canoes wearing only their baby-doll pyjamas. Some girls were famous for sneaking out of parties at Suydam's and skinny-dipping at the back beach.

ONE WONDERS WHAT THESE BOYS WERE AIMING AT IN 1951.

The 1960s: Gale Harild

IN OUR NECK OF THE BAY, INSIDE HELL'S GATE, OUR ROAD TO freedom was off-limits until we were ten. Only then were we considered old enough to handle the perils of motorboating through this treacherous passage. Water levels were low in the sixties and sheared pins were a common occurrence. By age ten, however, we were artful navigators. When the oldest of our communal family (Bennetts and Springers) reached the age of initiation, we were permitted to take our five horsepower through Hell's Gate and eventually to Whalen's to "meet the boat." We were always recognizable in our little green boat with its old pale-green Johnson 5 horsepower, which we later

WHAT WERE THEY TALKING ABOUT ALL THOSE NIGHTS AT THE GENGE'S?

HANGING OUT AT TOWNSEND ISLAND IN 1942 (LEFT).

164

The Regatta

FOR DECADES, BEGINning in 1925, the regatta has been the ultimate event of every Cognashene summer . . . at least for the young and competitive at heart. In the beginning, this annual Civic Holiday celebration was held at the Government dock at Whalen's Island. The adults would attend in masquerade costumes and anchor their boats offshore—the best vantage point for viewing the fun and games. Paddling and swimming were the main events, of course, but the grand finale in those early years was an awesome display of high-board diving.

Later, when the boat traffic increased, the regatta changed venues several times, and the events themselves evolved. There was the period of tilting—boy standing precariously on the gunnels, girl paddling frantically in the stern. There was "diving for dinner plates"—hardly an Olympic event, but terrific for its entertainment value.

The Cognashene regatta has had it all: excitement, competition, and, sadly, even a little danger. The "egg-bluff race" of the 1970s was promptly discontinued when contestants jumping off a cliff landed on the heads (and various other body parts) of contestants already in the water, as was the ill-advised motorboat race of 1938, when a participant fell overboard and sustained a serious, propeller-related injury.

On the brighter side, several lighthearted events have helped to relieve the tension of the fierce, if friendly, competition. Some of the more serious regatta contenders condition themselves for weeks in advance, particularly

A REGATTA SIDESHOW IN THE LATE FORTIES,
COURTESY OF TED VOKES AND KEN WILSON.

with a view to winning the "canoe fives." This is the Holy Grail of the regatta set, the Stanley Cup of canoeing. The red ribbon won in that contest is one of the most prized among the array of regatta ribbons that have a special place on all Cognashene cottage walls.

FINE TILTING TECHNIQUE AT THE 1945 REGATTA.

called "Smell-my-hand." (I can still remember the gassy smell of that motor.) Our old Johnson, although reliable, had no reverse and the tiny tank at the top of the engine had to be filled before every trip. It was always a little embarrassing to row out of the docks at Whalen's or to ask Rob Gropp or Peter McGibbon to fill 'er up. (That cost about ten cents in those days with a special mixture of 16 to 1.)

Our parents, of course, loved that safe boat. We did a lot of bonding on those trips to the store: A boatload of kids would take about an hour each way—we certainly had lots of time to talk.

The 1960s: Sandra McGugan

AS YOUNG CHILDREN, OUR ACTIVITIES WERE LIMited by how far we could walk or paddle, and we beat a well-trodden path to our grandparents' cottage around our bay. When we were feeling particularly adventurous, we would walk across to "houseboat island," climb through the windows of the *Vancrofter*, and explore the "haunted" interior.

Our social life centred around the swimming program which we attend-

ed regularly, and the daily trip to the store at Whalen's to buy comic books and ice cream and to check for mail. (We rarely got mail but it was essential to check for it each and every day.) As we grew older and began to navigate tin boats with 9.9 motors we'd venture further afield, and of course, on windy days, that meant Aunt Edna's Island to swim in the pounding waves.

Canoe trips were another summer highlight—a chance to get away from parents, if only for a night or two. The food was always terrible, we got little sleep, and we complained loudly at every portage, but we wouldn't have missed them for anything.

The 1970s: Susan McGibbon

JACQUELINE BISSET, FRED FLINTSTONE, SHIRLEY TEMple and the Hulk may seem like unlikely characters to meet at a party or share a dance with at the cottage, but during a few special summers in Cognashene, anything was possible.

The era of costume parties—a modern spin on the long-standing tradition of charades—was born in the early seventies as a certain group of teens sought more and more inventive ways of having fun. While the themes of these parties tended to vary, imagination, a strong sense of

The Sixties Unfold

Halfway between the introduction of organized fun, under the auspices of the JCCA with its bonfire/picnicking emphasis, and the present day, a transition began in the mid-sixties. Cottage parties grew in popularity, and parents regularly appointed "older young people" to chaperone the boisterous gatherings. Primarily, the teens were engaged to watch over the younger ones as they played and splashed

around in the water, but they gradually assumed more responsibility. Thus the Cognashene Recreation Program was born.

From its small beginnings in the area of informal swimming, the concept expanded to embrace organized lessons in canoeing, sailing, crafts and, eventually, overnight camping trips. Today, Kirby's Beach on Arthurs' Island is still home base and the program is among the largest and best of its kind in Georgian Bay.

THE SMALL, SAFE GREEN RUNABOUT POWERED BY "SMELL-MY-HAND" (ABOVE). A SWIMMING CLASS IN THE SUMMER OF 1976 (BELOW).

impropriety and kegs of beer were always essential.

There were come-as-your-favourite-drink parties, where martinis, daiquiris, and brown cows mixed, so to speak, with Bloody Caesars, Black Russians, and other assorted liquid libations. There were come-as-your-favourite-TV-character evenings, when Radar O'Reilly, Superman and the Man from Glad mingled with the Wizard of Oz (dressed, oddly enough, in the sexiest rose-coloured robe ever seen on the Bay!). There were come-as-your-favourite-fantasy parties, which. . .well, maybe those are better left to the imagination. Suffice it to say, it's amazing what was created from a little bubble wrap, plastic fruit

and that old moo-moo that, if truth be known, you really wished your mother wouldn't wear anymore.

Entire summers followed a theme—the Toga year, the Punk Rock year, the Socks and Sunglasses year—but we never tired of the Beatles and Motown, or of the hilarity of unscrewing someone's gasoline hose, or removing a shearing pin.

We were young, it was Cognashene and we had fun.

The 1980s: Carol Webb

AT A VERY EARLY AGE, THIS PLACE BECAME homebase for me. My Cognashene friends are among my best friends. They, and our other cottage guests, tend to be the kinds of people who love the uniqueness of our particular Georgian Bay experience. They have to like sitting up all night in our fishbowl of a living room to watch the lightning work its way around our point of land as it moves from west to east, to share in the excitement of the elements because they really are different at Georgian Bay.

I think I become a different person when I'm at the Bay. I have my little rituals like dipping my toes in the water first thing after arriving, and removing my watch for the duration of my stay. At the start of every season, I sit

(LEFT TO RIGHT) J. KEOGH, H. KINNEAR, S. HENDERSON, AND A. CLARK IN 1993.

on the stone bench on our northern exposure absorbing the surroundings through my pores, anticipating the summer ahead. And I begin to lose my inhibitions. I sometimes think that may have something to do with the fact that we always wave to people when we pass them in our boats. . . .

I know we make a joke of it, but when we think we might be getting seri-

ous about someone, having them "up to the cottage" in order to gauge their response to our island life is an essential step in determining if a lasting relationship is worthwhile.

The 1990s:
Christina Crabtree (age 10)

I WAS AT MY WARM, COSY COTTAGE IN ONTARIO, CANADA, with my family. It was the summertime and we were there on vacation. I had been waiting to go all year. On Wednesday morning I jumped out of bed: Tonight we were going to my cousin's and the only way to get there was by boat. All day we prepared to go, and when it was time to leave for their place, everyone got into their tight, uncomfortable life jackets, and we all scrambled into the boat. I untied the sturdy ropes and abruptly pushed off. I sat with the wind and cool water blowing in my face.

When we finally got there, I ran up to their cottage and pulled the heavy door open. I stepped inside and smelled the scent of a succulent dinner cooking and sweet, fresh blueberry pie. My aunt told me that she had made it that afternoon from berries picked on the island. My cousins and I set the table and then gathered everyone around. I was so excited, I could barely eat.

That night we were going to see a comet shower and fireworks. When it was time, we walked outside and lay down on our backs. We started looking up at the beautiful sky. The cool night breeze was blowing and I thought about how lucky I was to have the family I have and to have all kinds of relatives who care for me. I never wanted that cool night to end.

Soon afterwards, we had to go home, but I will never forget that evening.

POWER AND GLORY

THE NATURE OF COGNASHENE

IN COGNASHENE, THE PLEASURE, JOY AND DELIGHT OF ITS wind, water, rocks and sky must be tempered by the knowledge that it can also be a dangerous and even cruel place. The beast never lurks far beneath the breathtaking beauty. A bright, balmy day can suddenly take a vengeful turn. The wild pink roses may harbour a massasauga rattler. The glistening sculptured rocks can become jagged shoals that will sink a ship. The graceful deer leaps through the forest but the wolf isn't far behind.

It is not everybody's cup of tea. Some visitors are alarmed by the rugged, exposed isolation of the place. But for those who are hooked, it is the blatant immodesty of nature and the challenge it holds for the inhabitants that are the magnets which draw them to Cognashene year after year.

Flora

ABOUT 20,000 YEARS AGO AS THE ICE AGE RETREATED, THE SOIL was scraped from the rocks of Georgian Bay leaving them even more exposed than they are today. Then the lichen, the pioneer of all growth on the islands, took hold after some millennia. This plant is a composite life-form combining algae and fungi in one crusty and pervasive covering. It is dependent on the rock for its growth. Today we see lichen of pure gold

thanks to this rich carpet of green that the rocks are alive with growth of all colours and sensation, including lowly lichens, waving grasses, brilliant blossoms, prickly junipers and ultimately, the Bay's crowning glory, the white pine.

Yellow sedum is a new plant on the rocks and its distinctive brilliance in the spring is astounding. It is expanding at a great rate and covering more and more of the granite as its spores drift on the wind. The tiny flowers change to emerald green in the summer. Sedum, too, owes its life to the nurturing nature of lichen.

Why is it so difficult to grow a rose in one's garden in the city when they thrive in the thin soil on the rocks of Georgian Bay? Nodding pink wild roses adorn the smallest islands in July and August. Pin cherry, black cherry and an assortment of berry blossoms brighten May and June.

For those who are lucky enough to be on the islands right after the ice is out, wild orchids, violets, the twin leaf (a plant that's stunning for its solitary white flower), and a variety of other wee flowers can be seen popping up deep in the bush. Yellow lady's slipper and the purplish-brown or green Jack-in-the-pulpit bide their time until late June. August brings us the startling red cardinal flower by the water's edge. Other wildflowers seem to come and go each year as their seeds blow about from one mossy and grey-green—muted tints that enhance the natural colours of the granite.

The lush green moss that beds the bushes followed the lichens in greening the islands. It supplies much-needed nutrients for the germination of seeds. It's crevasse to another and from one island to the next.

The wonderful marketing of wildflower seeds has spread the beauty of unknown flowers to Cognashene. *Gaillardia,* or blanketflower, a showy member of the daisy family with its large yellow flower, appeared on a septic bed one year. Viper's bugloss brightened the bank of soil on an abandoned leaching pit another year. Happy daisies spring up here and there every year with wanton carelessness and great variety. Mother Nature is the final arbiter.

Trees: Beating the Odds

COGNASHENERS ARE PROUD OF THEIR WARM AND COLOURFUL Precambrian rocks, but this lovely variegated surface is being covered over with green. There has been exponential growth of mosses, bushes and trees in the past century. A bed of moss will nurture a juniper seed or a few berry seeds dropped by the birds. These bushes mature and shelter the growth of a young pine or cedar. . .and so a forest grows. The hardy trees stand alone,

THE VARIEGATED SURFACE OF THE PRECAMBRIAN SHIELD IS THE HARDEST KNOWN ROCK IN THE WORLD.

RED SKY AT NIGHT: A MESMERIZING SUMMER SUNSET (ABOVE). SUMACH (BELOW) WILL COLOUR COGNASHENE IN FALL.

defiant in the face of nature's violence.

The white pine is the most common evergreen on the islands. It is the subject painters have chosen for generations to paint in its now familiar form, bending southeastward in backward obeisance to the northwest wind. Red pine, eastern hemlock, balsam fir, tamarack, white and black spruce and white and red cedar, all choose their particular sites on the islands.

Hard and soft woods compete for space in the limited acreage and soil available. Maples, birches, poplars and oaks are a few of the many deciduous trees that colour fall days with crimson, orange, yellow, and purple, contrasting the greens of the coniferous forests.

As well, there is a wonderful variety of wild fruit trees and bushes with an occasional apple tree gone wild. Sour chokecherries have more appeal to the birds than the cottagers, but it's a fight to the finish for the sweet fruits: blueberries, huckleberries, blackberries, elderberries, sarsaparilla and dozens of others which fill cottagers' pies and freezers.

Wild Things to Eat

YOU WILL NEVER GO HUNGRY IN COGNASHENE IF YOU have access to 100 acres of woodland. In early spring the clintonia or corn lily appears. Its three pale green pointed leaves add a refreshing cucumber flavour to a salad.

Add some young dandelion leaves for a spring tonic.

As the season progresses, watch for the Solomon's seal. Its long taproot, parboiled, is delicious and resembles a water chestnut in flavour. The bulrush has many uses, the early shoots and blossoms make fine vegetables. The pollen in the cattail makes a tasty flour which can be used in baking with other flours.

GAILLARDIA, OR BLANKETFLOWER: A SHOWY MEMBER OF THE DAISY FAMILY.

Milkweed, wild leeks, acorns, water lilies, wild lettuce and many others along with berries and fruits are all good fun to gather and healthy to eat. There is a wonderful variety of mushrooms available to the adventurous spirit, but two or three species are poisonous. Gather wisely and carry a reference book.

Drinks, Anyone?

WHEN YOU ARE THIRSTY FOR SOMETHING MORE EXOTIC THAN delicious Georgian Bay water, rest assured your options are endless. Wild mint grows abundantly and makes a refreshing cup of tea. In the fall, gather the vitamin C-rich rosehips that have turned a beautiful hew of fiery red. Use them in tea to give your immune system a boost. Dandelion roots, gathered in the early summer, dried and ground, make a healthy coffee substitute. Blueberry leaves and their related species, picked in early spring, are full of nutrition when steeped in boiling water for five minutes. They can be dried for future use, too. Cranberries make juice, elderberries make wine, white cedar bark makes tea that is full of vitamin C. So, what'll it be?

Fauna

WILDLIFE IN COGNASHENE VARIES FROM THOSE TINY ants which find their way into sugar bowls to large black bears which can find their way into refrigerators. The different species will vary not just from season to season, but from year to year, from decade to decade and from century to century.

Survival of the fittest is the law of the predatory and territorial animals and birds.

Mammals, Scarce but Friendly

SUMMER COTTAGERS AND VISITORS TO COGNASHENE may encounter only one or two indigenous animals during a vacation. Most of the local creatures are never seen at all. However, the ubiquitous raccoon nests on any island where garbage is generated. They can survive on the natural flora and fauna (berries and grubs make a nutritious meal), but prefer to have their dinner served up for them in the compost heap, the garden, the garbage bin or even on the kitchen table.

While raccoons are around every year some years more than others produce large numbers of mice, moles, voles, and flying and red squirrels. These creatures will try to sneak into cottages for some warmth and free food. But there is a cycle to these animals—when there are lots of predators afoot, the numbers decline. Once again, nature is in control.

Some less common animals—beaver, muskrat, mink, otter and the very occasional weasel—may be glimpsed swimming along the water's edge. Beaver and muskrat are usually unwelcome around cottages. Muskrat will build their nests under docks and chew up the flotation Styrofoam. Beaver will build their lodge right inside the boathouse or will dam up the spring run-off, forming a pond in which to build a lodge.

Cottagers have been known to knock down a dam to save the trees that suffer when the water level rises too high. But if they choose to pursue this course of action, they must be persistent. Canada's national animal will beaver away all night to rebuild what mere mortals have dislodged. Two weeks of constant destruction may discourage the industrious beaver and finally send him on his way.

On the larger islands one might flush partridge or ruffed grouse out of the bush. Rabbits and hares also live in the bush, but are more visible in the winter by their tracks. And where there are game birds and rabbits there will be a friendly red fox controlling the population. Of course, porcupines and skunks are ever present, though they prefer to maintain a low profile. It's not at all uncommon for pet dogs to sniff them out of their protective lairs. Black bears will make their presence known during a summer of drought or following a spring with a late frost. They will swim from one island to the next in search of berries or whatever they might find in the garbage.

In winter, white-tailed deer cross over from the mainland to the islands in search of food; to glimpse one is truly a treat. Their presence will bring wolves during the coldest months.

It Had to be Snakes...

EVERYONE HAS A LOVE OR HATE RELATIONSHIP WITH SNAKES. WITH ten species on the islands of Cognashene, cottagers have a great choice on which to exercise their emotions. Most prominent and least-loved is the massasauga rattlesnake, the only poisonous snake in Ontario. Due to the often wanton and sometimes defensive killing of this small member of the rattler family it is designat-

THE EASTERN HOGNOSED SNAKE IS ONLY A THREAT TO NESTING BIRDS.

ed an endangered species.

That said, this reptile holds a dear place in the hearts of many Cognasheners who are known to affectionately declare a hot sunny day a "rattlesnake day," in honour of the fact that this is when the snakes slither out of their moist swampy areas to enjoy a sunbath on the hot rocks.

A program to protect this threatened species on Beausoleil Island, and many stories of benign encounters, have achieved a certain acceptance of the rattlesnake, enabling it to share the islands more peacefully.

Some other varieties include the northern water snake, garter, fox, and the ring-necked and eastern hognosed snakes. None of these is dangerous to people or pets but they are a threat to nesting birds. Not only can snakes invade the nests of shorebirds but they have been found in nests high up in the trees devouring eggs or chicks. The fox snake can grow up to six feet in length and has a voracious appetite. A large one once made the mistake of trying to swallow a mud puppy, tail first. The frantic mud puppy whipped its head around and bit the snake, but since neither was winning (or losing) the battle, a helping hand extricated the mud puppy and the snake slid away hungry.

Frogs, toads, bullfrogs and tree toads, those wonder-

PINK WILD ROSES EXUDE A DELICATE CHARM.

ful creatures that serenade campers and cottagers in the evenings of early summer, populate Cognashene's shores and islands. The blue-tailed skink is still alive and well in the area, as is the mud puppy.

The map turtle is the most common of the seven or eight species of turtles found in Cognashene and can often be seen sunning itself on a log out in the Bay. How the eggs ever hatch, or how the babies ever reach the water, is a mystery.

The spotted turtle is a threatened species. Its population declined dramatically in the 1950s but is slowly growing again thanks to a research project on Beausoleil Island. Snapping turtles are rare but still around, no doubt due to the abundance of ducklings in the spring.

Shore Things

WHAT A REMARKABLE BIRD THE TERN IS AND A BEAUTIFUL SIGHT TO behold. Its ability to dive from great heights straight into the depths of the bay and capture its prey in its beak makes for a dramatic display. The common tern competes with the gulls in the inland bays, while the larger Caspian tern, which nests on the Watchers, is more often seen on the outer islands. A Caspian tern was recently seen diving into the water. When it emerged it took flight with some difficulty with a large black creature dan-

gling from its beak. A second or two later it dropped its prey. Then, a loon appeared in the water shaking its head, dazed as if it had been struck with something. A strong beak perhaps? And then, to the rescue, arrived two other loons in flight chasing the unfortunate tern. Any creature can make a mistake.

The herring gulls have been the most common shorebird in the area but their numbers are decreasing. Although they are scavengers, they feed on a variety of marine animals as well as berries. Sometimes one can be seen dropping a clam onto the rocks to break it open. Before a storm their raucous cries fill the air as they fly back to their nests against the wind.

Until recently, the ring-billed gull had been only an occasional visitor but its population is increasing. Fishermen delight in throwing the heads and guts of the fish they have cleaned to the gulls, leaving the remains on the shore as an hors d'oeuvre for the latecomers.

The most graceful bird to enhance the shores is without a doubt the great blue heron. It can be seen taking off slowly and ponderously from the edge of a pond or an inlet where it feeds on frogs and fish.

The fish-eating common merganser, with its long, slender, slightly hooked bill, is a more familiar sight than any other duck in Cognashene. Early July and sometimes again in mid-August, a mother duck appears around the shores of the islands with her dozen or more ducklings swim-

TAKING FLIGHT: THE MALE COMMON MERGANSER (IN THE LEAD) IS MARKED BY HIS GLOSSY BLACKISH-GREEN HEAD AND UPPER NECK; THE FEMALE, WITH A TYPICALLY CRESTED, TAWNY BROWN HEAD, FOLLOWS.

ming along behind. Mallards are seen on occasion feeding on aquatic plants around the shores.

The call of the loon is heard more often now than in the past. Their population, along with so many other shorebirds, was decimated by DDT and acid rain in the forties and fifties, but their comeback is heralded by a most welcome sound.

Canada geese will occasionally nest around the shores but are more likely to be seen and heard on their migration route. Hurray for the return of the osprey. In the early seventies, a pair of nesting osprey were sighted on the hydro pole on Hedley's Island, the first ever to be seen by the residents there. Perhaps the osprey left the Cognashene area after all the tall pine trees had been logged in the 1880s, leaving nothing high enough for them to call home.

Today, the Osprey Association guards the interests of this slowly increasing population. Members count the number of ospreys seen in their area annually, and will erect a twenty-foot pole on a site considered suitable for a nesting pair to build on. What a tragedy if they should disappear for good;

it is a spectacular sight to watch them swoop and soar and catch their prey. They descend onto the surface of the water, clutch a fish in their waiting talons and slowly rise in the air, borne aloft by their six-foot wingspan.

Pesticides devastated the double-crested cormorant during the first half of this century. By 1950 only 1,000 nesting pairs remained. In the past fifteen years their numbers have increased to such an extent that many cottagers, worried about the depletion of sport fish in the area, are asking the government to cull the population.

Birds of Various Feathers

THE ISLANDS' FLORA AND VARIED INSECT LIFE ATTRACT many species of migrating birds. One-hundred-and-twenty have been identified on Burnt Island alone. Most commonly seen and heard during July and August are the song sparrow, yellow-rumped warbler and red-eyed vireo, though many others serenade sunbathers on the rocks. Swallows provide constant motion around every cottage as they swoop and dive after flies. Even prairie warblers hang about, far off their usual flight path, but seemingly enamoured of Cognashene, as they return year after year to nest. Each spring since about 1988 the whippoorwill sounds his call after a long hiatus. Hawks are more frequent visitors these days and turkey vultures have recently made their debut in Cognashene. In winter, many birds remain and feed on the lingering berries which bring colour and life to the white, still world of winter.

Things That Creep and Crawl

SUFFICE IT TO SAY, THE PLACE IS CRAWLING WITH THEM. MOSQUITOES, flies, bees, hornets, wasps, spiders, butterflies, dragonflies, moths and millions of others are all here in Cognashene. They supply food for birds, fish and frogs, and are the chief pollinators of berry bushes and wildflowers. But cedar bugs (sometimes coyly referred to as wood bugs or even cockroaches): Are they really so necessary? Blackflies, so common on the mainland, seldom appear on the outer islands but when they do they are vicious. The monarch butterflies stop in Cognashene on their pilgrimage south, always a welcome sight and a benign presence. Which makes them most

THE BULLFROG: A COMMON ENOUGH SIGHT IN ANY LILY POND.

unlike *Schistosome cercaria*, a nasty parasite which is hosted by ducks, gulls and snails in the water, and ultimately, human skin. The resulting "swimmers' itch" is an unpleasant condition which can be avoided by towelling dry after swimming.

The gypsy moth tyrannized Cognashene for three long years. It wreaked havoc on the oak trees and some maples, birches and pines, but fortunately, Mother Nature stepped in at the critical moment bringing a heavy late frost in May 1992. This killed the larvae before they hatched and could begin munching on the new spring leaves.

Tent caterpillars threaten the lives of cherry trees every once in a while. They will appear for three or four years in a row and then disappear for several years. The hardy fruit trees seem to survive after each onslaught and continue to produce fruit for the wildlife.

Fish and Fisherfolk

DURING THE NINETEENTH CENTURY, FISH WERE SO PLENTIFUL around the shores of the Bay that commercial fishermen harvested from spring breakup straight through to December. With their large nets they

AN EERIE CALM AFTER THE STORM.

hauled in many tons of herring, lake trout and sturgeon, three species which are now extinct or rare in our waters.

Today, sportfishing enthusiasts come to Cognashene to catch smallmouth black bass, pickerel, pike and muskellunge, mainly. There are an unbelievable eighty species of fish in the waters of Cognashene, and many are frequently (perhaps too frequently) caught.

The rock bass is the most pernicious and unwelcome fish to be pulled in, while the sunfish is probably the prettiest. Small perch will take a worm too.

A new fish in Cognashene's waters is the kokanee salmon, introduced to the Bay in the 1960s. It is a great sport fish as well as good eating. Catfish, dogfish, carp and suckers, all bottom feeders, are not welcome catches, although they don't taste so bad to hungry fisherfolk after a long, unsuccessful day on the water.

The Elements

THE COMBINATION OF AIR AND WATER IS A VOLATILE ONE IN Cognashene. Stories of boaters stranded—or worse—in a squall are not unusual. Ten-foot waves are common at the height of a storm. These can knock floating docks off their pinnings, dismantle cribs under permanent docks, untie boats, drag moorings down the bay and sweep cabins off their foundations. Water levels have been known to rise or fall three feet in an hour depending on the direction of the wind.

Cottages that have withstood storms for many decades can be smashed apart or swept away by one ferocious gust of wind. A cottage exposed to the northwest wind for forty years virtually exploded in 1994 when the wind broke a window and entered the cottage with such force it blew the walls apart. Forces of nature can and will overcome man's ingenuity. Now cottagers have their cabins attached to the rock with strong metal cables—the kind that can attract lightening.

Gusts of wind that often exceed sixty miles an hour take down trees indiscriminately. One Tree Island lost its tree of long-standing and is now No Tree Island. Trees in general have little soil in which to anchor themselves, but the roots have adapted to finding crevasses and boulders into which they can twine. The taller they grow the more susceptible they are. However, in nature everything recycles itself, and rotting wood contributes to a rich humus soil for subsequent growth.

A good Georgian Bay storm is never complete without the driving horizontal rain that can find its way into the most airtight and waterproof structure. Or it can come straight down by the bucketful for a half-hour or more. Then, suddenly, it is over. The rocks are clean and have a warm, wet smell, the blueberry bushes are well-watered and the pines can enjoy another week of heat when their mossy beds are full of rainwater.

And so Cognasheners continue to endure these storms, and to survive to tell the tales of how they outlasted nature's powerful forces once again.

A SMALLMOUTH BASS MEASURES UP NICELY.

THE OFTEN EXTREME CONDITIONS OF A GEORGIAN BAY STORM ARE NOT TO EVERYONE'S TASTE, BUT THEY MAKE FOR A DRAMATIC DISPLAY.

Acknowledgements

MANY PEOPLE PARTICIPATED IN THE CREATION OF *Wind, Water, Rock and Sky*, generously sharing with us their time, talents, and knowledge. It was their undying passion for a place called Cognashene that was the driving force throughout the complex and lengthy process of creating this book.

First and foremost, a wholehearted thank you to Duggan Melhuish, who conceived of the idea to create a book, and also to all those who painstakingly researched and wrote the chapters. *Wind, Water, Rock and Sky* is truly their labour of love.

Thanks in general go to the CCA Board, Bill Davis, John Denison, Wally King and Alistair Melhuish for their enthusiastic encouragement in the early stages, when the idea to publish a book seemed but a risky vision. We also acknowledge the financial leadership of Larry Ward; the support and conceptual guidance of Francess Halpenny, Liz Lundell, Paul McMahon and Judy Ross; the publishing and marketing advice of Brian Clark, Joyce Cole, Russell Floren, Jamie Hunter, curator, Huronia Museum, Barry McDougall and Mike Wallace; the patience and good faith of Fred Cheetham on behalf of our printer, Friesens; the production expertise of Jeff Ostilly; the knowledgeable assistance of Hilary Lawrence and Bill Smith of Huronia Museum, during our photography sessions there; the research assistance of Terri Preece; the editing assistance of Sue Russell; the helpful feedback of Alison, Eleanor and Merfyn David; and the good natured support and creative eyes of Hans Engell and Daniel Zimerman.

During the summer of 1996, the book's photography and styling team visited Longuissa and Franceville, and for their kind reception at that time we thank the Cooper and Simon families, respectively.

Wind, Water, Rock and Sky is privately published, and as such was only made possible with the generous financial support of many Cognashene friends and organizations. We are grateful for the donations made in the name of the Cognashene Cottagers' Association and the Cognashene Community Church.

In addition, many donations were made in loving memory of friends now departed. Fondly remembered in this way are Sue Shoemaker Allison, Marion and Ted Bowden, Ernest Ford Howard and Zina Hope McCarthy, William (Bill) Mathews, Dorothy and Ivan Melhuish, Dr. Walter and Harriet Sutton, Ruth Wilson.

We are also grateful to the following, whose generous investments provided the working capital for this book: Craig A. Bowden and Family, Lydia and Jim Bowden, Jean and Bob Butler, Betsy and Andrew Clark, Brian Clark and Johanne Smart, Maureen and Jim Cooper, Louise and Bill Dimma, Joanne and Pat Edwards, Lawrence Heisey, Helen and Murphy Hull, Laureen and Bob Kinnear, George Ledingham, Dorothy E. and William G. Leonard, Mr. and Mrs. John L. McCarthy and Family, Alistair and Duggan Melhuish, Sue and Bruce Melhuish, Jean, Margot, Patrick, Scott and Christina Northey, Vivian and Doug Smith, Harriet and Gord Walker, Judy and Larry Ward, Joan and Alan G. Watson, Margaret and Colin G. Watson, and Joyce and Dave Winlo.

For her ability to wear so many hats so well (creative, marketing, production), Susan McGibbon deserves special mention. And finally, our sincere thanks are due to all those "Cognasheners" too numerous to mention, but who nevertheless offered their memories, family photos, stories and support throughout. We hope you enjoy the result of this uniquely collaborative effort.

THE BOOK TEAM

Acknowledgements

The Creative Team

BACK ROW, FROM LEFT TO RIGHT:

Neil Asselin, Stylist

Marta Cutler

Michael Kohn, Photographer

FRONT ROW, FROM LEFT TO RIGHT:

Carol Moskot, Designer and Art Director

Susan McGibbon

Jennifer David, Editor

The Book Team

CLOCKWISE, FROM BACK LEFT-HAND CORNER:

Alistair Melhuish, Bill Endress,

Jim Bowden, Pat Edwards,

Duggan Melhuish, Larry Ward,

Dave Winlo, Rolfe Jones,

Marta Cutler, Christopher Baines,

Jane Loughborough,

Sue Russell, Susan McGibbon

Chapter Notes

A concerted effort has been made to acknowledge all sources of information, which are listed below in the chapter notes when not previously mentioned in the narrative.

IN THE BEGINNING

NATIVE ROOTS

By Peter H. Russell

With thanks to members of the Beausoleil First Nation who generously gave of their time, and to Jim Morrison for his reading of this chapter. Chapter icon: Christian Island quill box.

SOURCES

1. Rogers, Edward S., and Smith, Donald B. Ed. *Aboriginal Ontario, Historical Perspectives on the First Nations*. p. 48

2. Cranston, J. Herbert. *Huronia: Cradle of Ontario's History*. Quoting from Champlain's journal; p. 5

3. Rogers, Edward S., and Smith, Donald B. Ed. *Aboriginal Ontario, Historical Perspectives on the First Nations*. p. 56

4. Dickason, Olive Patricia. *Canada's First Nations, A History of Founding Peoples from Earliest Times*. p. 131

5. Cranston, J. Herbert. *Huronia: Cradle of Ontario's History*. p. 80

6. Schmalz, Peter S. *The Ojibwa of Southern Ontario*. p. 25

7. Rogers, Edward S., and Smith, Donald B. Ed. *Aboriginal Ontario: Historical Perspectives on the First Nations*. p.112

8. Slattery, Brian. *The Land Rights of Indigenous Canadian Peoples*.

9. Ibid.

10. Ibid.

11. Ibid.

12. Ibid.

MUSKOKA MILLS

By Owen T. Jones

With thanks to Arthur Norton. Chapter icon: authentic lumber workers' tools.

SOURCES

1. Cross, Michael S. *The Lumber Community of Upper Canada 1815 – 1867*. p. 213

2. Ibid., p. 216

3. MacKay, Donald. *The Lumberjacks*. p. 9

4. Ibid., p. 8

5. Murray, Florence B. Ed. *Muskoka and Haliburton 1615 – 1875*. p. 1ii

6. Ibid.; in Alexander Murray's report to Wm. E. Logan (provincial geologist) for the year 1853, p. 159

7. Angus, James T. *A Deo Victoria*. p. 143

8. Ibid., p. 137

9. Muskoka Mill & Lumber Company, Directors Minute Book, August 1, 1877, p. 6

10. Ibid., Directors Minute Book, August 5, 1880, p. 14

11. The Ontario Provincial Directory of 1886–1887.

12. *Free Press Herald*, Midland, April 28, 1954, quoting the *Toronto Free World*, August 8, 1889

13. Ibid.

PIONEER DAYS

By Jane Loughborough and Alistair Melhuish

With thanks to Dora Louise Smith Halpenny. Additional information: The *Cognashene Cottager*, 1967, 1968. Chapter icon: tour pamphlets.

SOURCES

1. Berchem, F. R. *The Yonge Street Story (1793 – 1860)*. Toronto, Natural Heritage/Natural History Inc., 1996. p. 19

2. Smith, Stephen. "Yonge at Heart," *Canadian Geographic* magazine. September/October, 1996. p. 28

3. Ibid. p. 28

4. Berchem, F. R. *The Yonge Street Story (1793 – 1860)*. p. 35

5. Ibid. p. 24

6. Cranston, Herbert J. *Huronia: Cradle of Ontario's History*. Barrie, Simcoe County Historical Association. p. 61 – 63

GETTING THERE

By Jim Bowden

Chapter icon: the steering wheel from Franceville's *Sagamo 2*.

SPECIAL PLACES

LONGUISSA

By Renata Humphries

With many thanks to Mary Byers, whose fine book *Longuissa* (The Boston Mills Press, Erin, Ontario, 1988) was a great and entertaining source of information for this chapter, and also to Elizabeth Bell.

Credit is also due to Vincent Massey, whose book *What's Past is Prologue: The Memoirs of the Right Honourable Vincent Massey* (Toronto, 1963) is quoted here, and to H. T. Meek, author of *Archibald Campbell and His Family* (Toronto, 1959) and *Leighton Goldie McCarthy and his Wife, Muriel Drummond Campbell* (Toronto, 1954). Chapter icon: original Longuissa dinner bell.

FRANCEVILLE
By Duggan Melhuish
With thanks to Guy and Kathy Johnstone, Ernie Howard, Jamie Hunter and Bill Smith of the Huronia Museum, Midland, Muriel and Bert Thompson (for their excellent "Franceville History"), The Diary Of Fanny France, the Journals Of Winnie France, and the following issues of the *Cognashene Cottager*: 1967, 1968, 1969, 1970, and 1982. Chapter icon: wall sconce from one of the two hotels.

WHALEN'S
By Valerie Wilson
With thanks to Helen Zoschke, Robert Gropp. Chapter icon: original Cocking Island mailbox.

MINNICOGNASHENE
By Sue Russell and Bill Deeks
With thanks to Bob Jarvis. Icon: postcards.

BLARNEY CASTLE
By Duggan Melhuish
With thanks to Dr. Jim Cooper, John and Bernice Cooper and Lorna Kruger.

CHURCH ON THE ROCKS
By Duggan Melhuish
With thanks to Reverend Herb Breithaupt (whose writings in the United Church *Observer* helped to set the tone), Reverend Wendy MacFadzean (whose sermons served to inspire), and the following for their input: David Reade, Bob Kinnear, Ruth Langley, Fred Beattie, Marion Bowden and Dr. Harold Hedley.

LOCAL LEGENDS
AUNT EDNA BREITHAUPT
By Duggan Melhuish
With thanks to Susan Bellingham of the Dora Lewis Rare Book Room (home of the Breithaupt-Hewetson-Clark archives) at the University Of Waterloo, Waterloo, Ontario, Dorothy Leonard, Tillie Bennett, Ruth Langley, Miro Mesesnel, Russell Hewetson and Herb Breithaupt.

BILLY BRISSETTE
By Pat Cosman
With thanks to George Dubé.

WILF FRANCE
By Duggan Melhuish

ALBERT KING
By David Dupuis
With thanks to Rita Larmand, Richard Larmand, Sue (Larmand) Gignac, Nancy (Swales) Pilon, Patrick Dupuis, Alvin Dupuis, Anne Gagne.

CELESTE ROBITAILLE
By Duggan Melhuish
Based on interviews with Celeste and Dorothy Robitaille.

ORVILLE WRIGHT
By Duggan Melhuish
With thanks to Arthur Halpenny, Robert Haddler, Dearborn Museum (Detroit), Guy Johnstone and Wilkinson Wright. Chapter icon: Orville Wright's cheque for the purchase of Lambert Island.

REFLECTIONS
WHEN WE WERE YOUNG
Introduction by Jack Beattie & Duggan Melhuish
Thanks also to: Leslie Allison, Chris Baines, Carolyn, Craig and Jim Bowden, Ian Ferguson, Helen Fitzgerald, Jane Loughborough, Sally Mead, Janet Murphy, Rebecca Sherman, Perrie Soth, Murray Vokes, and Nora Wilson (per Ruth Wilson). Chapter icon: ring-toss game, circa 1940s.

POWER AND GLORY
By Sue Russell
With thanks to Dr. Rick Miller. Additional information was found in the *Cognashene Cottager*, 1972 and 1983.

Art Credits

Every effort has been made to acknowledge the source of each piece of art in this book. We apologize in advance for any errors or omissions.

OLD PHOTO COLLECTIONS (Sources listed alphabetically) ARCHIVES OF ONTARIO: pp. 28–29 (C7 1-38), 31 (C7 1-36). BALWIN COLLECTION, Metro Toronto Reference Library: pp. 15 (T31616), 22 (T31254). JAMES BARRY: provided art research for Native Roots. PETER BELL: provided photo research for Longuissa chapter; pp. 68, 69, 72, 73, 75, 76. BOWDEN COLLECTION: pp. 58 (both), 59 (both), 60, 61, 62, 63. MARY BYERS (author) and HUGH ROBERTSON: granted permission to reprint photos from *Longuissa* (privately published in 1988 and printed by The Boston Mills Press): pp. 66–67, 73, 75, 76. RALPH BUTT: p. 97. CANADIAN PACIFIC ARCHIVES: p. 80 (upper right). COOPER FAMILY COLLECTION: pp. 39, 40, 48 (upper & lower left), 52 (upper), 56–57, 116–117, 118 (lower), 119, 124–125, 126, 127, 129, 130, 131, 158 (lower right), 162. DAVID DUPUIS: pp. 144, 145, 146. GALE HARILD: p. 168 (lower). HELEN FITZGERALD: p. 43 (right). RUSSELL HEWETSON: pp. 150, 152, 153, 161 (lower). HEWETSON/ CLARK/ BREITHAUPT ARCHIVES, University Of Waterloo: pp. 134–135, 137, 138. DOROTHY & JOHN HORWOOD: pp. 48 (lower right), 161 (upper). ERNEST HOWARD: p. 153—A.Y. Jackson Triptych (photographed by Carlo Catenazzi). HURONIA MUSEUM: pp. 18 (1990.0037.0034), 42 (both photos; upper, 1992. 0083.0094), 46 (1947.0144.0046), 47 (lower, 1989.0011.0044), 54 (1989. 0001.0053), 80 (lower right, 1989.0001.0171), 81 (1989.0001.0129), 84 (lower right, 1989.001.0140), 85 (upper, 1989.0001.0052; lower, 1989.0001. 0093), 88 (lower, 1989.0001.0110), 89 (1989.0002.0008), 115 (1996.0026. 0024), 140 (1989.0002.0058), 141 (1989.0001.0006), 143 (upper, 1989.0001. 0184). BOB IRONSIDE J.W. BALD POSTCARD COLLECTION: pp. 83 (upper left), 107 (lower right), 109 (upper right), 112 (upper left). OWEN JONES: p.33. DOROTHY LEONARD: pp. 26, 47 (upper), 60, 136 (both photos), 107 (upper right). MCGIBBON FAMILY: front cover, pp. 158 (upper, lower right), 159 (both), 165 (upper left), 178 (lower right). MELHUISH FAMILY: pp. 50 (both photos), 59, 118 (upper left), 112, 123 (both photos), 139, 156–157, 163 (lower right), 164 (upper, lower right), 165 (lower left). NATIONAL ARCHIVES OF CANADA: pp. 14 (C-85845), 16 (C-11661), 19 (C-26212), 41 (C-13183). NATIONAL GALLERY OF CANADA (and Dr. Naomi Jackson Groves who granted permission to reproduce the art): p. 153, A.Y. Jackson oils—March Storm, Georgian Bay (#5051), and Early Spring, Georgian Bay (#1813). BERNARD NICHOLSON: pp. 12–13. DOROTHY & CELESTE ROBITAILLE: pp. 147, 148, 149 (both photos). SUE RUSSELL: pp. 63, 98 –99, 100 (all items), 101, 107 (left), 108, 110, 111, 113, 114 (both), 115 (right). REBECCA SHERMAN: p. 51. PERRIE SOTH: pp. 168 (lower), 169. BERT THOMPSON: pp. 83 (lower right), 84 (top left), 88 (top left & right). TRINITY COLLEGE, University of Toronto: p. 43 (upper left). BOB WEEKES: pp. 143 (lower), 175. COLIN WATSON: p. 158 (left). VALERIE & BOB WILSON: pp. 90–91, 93, 95, 101, 164 (left).

CONTEMPORARY PHOTOGRAPHY
MICHAEL KOHN: all still life and icon photographs (which appear at the start of every chapter); pp. 17, 20, 21, 24, 25, 27, 32, 35, 36, 39, 52, 55, 70, 71, 74, 77, 82, 89, 94, 106, 120, 121, 160, 161, 166, and close-cropped images on pp. 167, 173, 174 and 175. GARY BREITHAUPT: pp. 173, 179. DICK CUTLER: back cover, pp. 7, 9, 88, 128, 170–171, 172 (both photos), 177. BOB JARVIS: pp. 175 (lower left), 176. THOMAS KITCHIN/FIRSTLIGHT: pp. 176. SUE RUSSELL: pp. 174, 175 (upper right).

ILLUSTRATIONS
FRED BECK: pp. 6, 8, 181, 182. W. PAUL HUGHES: pp. 180, 184, 188, 191. JOAN WATSON: p. 190.

ICON PHOTOGRAPHY
Contributions of items from the following enriched much of the still life and icon photography found throughout the book: PETER & CATHY COOPER; ROSE & IAN DAVIS; RUTH & NEIL DAVIS; SHIRLEY & LARRY SIMONS; BARBARA COOPER; DOUG & HOLLY COOPER; LAUREEN & BOB KINNEAR; J. B. JENNINGS; SUE RUSSELL; JIM BOWDEN; DUGGAN MELHUISH; WENDY MACFADZEAN; JOHN & BERNICE COOPER; DR. HAROLD & EMMELINE HEDLEY; LARRY WARD; SARA HENDERSON; SUSAN MCGIBBON; FRED BECK; CHRIS BAINES; NORA WILSON; REBECCA & CREIGHTON SHERMAN. In addition, the HURONIA MUSEUM and the MUSEUM AT DISCOVERY HARBOUR generously allowed our photography team access to their collections.

Bibliography

ANGUS, JAMES T. *A Deo Victoria: The Story of the Georgian Bay Lumber Company, 1871–1942*. Severn Publications Limited, Orillia, 1994 (Second Printing)

ARP, BARBARA, Ed. *Reflections*. An Historical Anthology of Collingwood. Corporation of the Town of Collingwood, 1983

BARRY, JAMES P. *Georgian Bay, The Sixth Great Lake*. Toronto, Clarke Irwin & Company Limited, 1983

BARRY, JAMES P. *Georgian Bay: An Illustrated History*. Toronto, Stoddart Publishing Co. Limited, 1992

BERCHEM, F.R. *The Yonge Street Story, 1793 – 1860*, An Account from Letters, Diaries and Newspapers. Natural Heritage/Natural History Inc., 1996

BRAZER, MARJORIE CAHN. *The Sweet Water Sea, A Guide to Lake Huron's Georgian Bay*. Heron Books, Manchester, Michigan, 1984

BROWN, RON. *Ghost Towns of Ontario*. Langley B.C., Stagecoach Publishing Co. Ltd., 1978

BYERS, MARY. *Longuissa*. Erin, Ontario, The Boston Mills Press, Privately printed, 1988

COOMBE, GERALDINE. *Muskoka Past and Present*. Toronto, McGraw-Hill Ryerson Limited, 1976

CROSS, MICHAEL S. *The Lumber Community of Upper Canada 1815 – 1867*. Ontario Historical Society, 1960

CRANSTON, J. HERBERT. *Huronia: Cradle of Ontario's History*. Simcoe County Historical Association. First published by the Huronia Historical Sites Association in 1949

DEFEBAUGH, JAMES ELLIOTT. *History of the Lumber Industry of America*. Chicago, The American Lumberman, 1906

DE GRUCHY, SUSAN. *Our Own Free World, The Human History of Beausoleil Island*. National Historic Sites Services, 1970

DE VISSER, JOHN, AND ROSS, JUDY. *Georgian Bay*. Toronto, The Boston Mills Press/Stoddart Publishing Co. Ltd., 1992

DICKASON, OLIVE PATRICIA. *Canada's First Nations: A History of Founding Peoples from Earliest Times*. Toronto, McClelland & Stewart Inc., 1992

FLOREN, RUSSELL, AND GUTSCHE, ANDREA. *Ghosts of the Bay: A Guide to the History of Georgian Bay*. Toronto, Lynx Images Inc., 1994

GUILLET, EDWIN C. *Early Days in Upper Canada*. Toronto, University of Toronto Press, 1933

HARTING, TONI. *French River: Canoeing the River of the Stick-Wavers*. The Boston Bills Press ,1996

HUGHES, BARRY C. *The Legend of Kitchikewana*. Midland, Midland-Penetang Free Press Herald, 1976

LEGGET, ROBERT E. *Railways of Canada*. Vancouver, Douglas & McIntyre Ltd., 1987

LONG, GARY. *This River the Muskoka*. Erin, Ontario, The Boston Mills Press, 1989.

MACFIE, JOHN. *Parry Sound: Logging Days*. Erin, Ontario, The Boston Mills Press, 1987

MACKAY, DONALD. *The Lumberjacks*. Montreal, McGraw-Hill Ryerson Limited, 1978

MEEK, HENRY T. *Archibald Hamilton Campbell 1819 – 1909 and His Family*. Toronto, Privately Printed, 1959

MORRISON, JAMES. *The Robinson Treaties of 1850, A Case Study*. Prepared for the Royal Commission on Aboriginal Peoples, Treaty and Land Research Section, 1993

ROGERS, EDWARD S., AND SMITH, DONALD B, ED. *Aboriginal Ontario: Historical Perspectives on the First Nations*. A publication of the Ontario Historical Studies Series for the Government of Ontario. Toronto, Dundern Press, 1994

ROURKE, JUANITA. *Up The Shore*. Midland, Up The Shore Enterprises and Midland Printers, 1995

SCHMALZ, PETER S. *The Ojibwa of Southern Ontario*. Toronto, University of Toronto Press, 1991

TRIGGER, BRUCE G. *The Indians and the Heroic Age of New France* (Revised Edition: 1989). The Canadian Historical Association, Historical Booklet No. 30

PERIODICALS AND OTHER SOURCES
CANADIAN GEOGRAPHIC magazine, July 1996
Various issues of the *Cognashene Cottager,* an annual publication of the Board of Directors of the Cognashene Cottagers' Association, Port Perry, Port Perry Printing Limited, 1949 to present
THE MUSKOKA SUN, "Lumbering in Muskoka," an historical series, 1979
THE FREE PRESS, Friday, February 8, 1974, "At Mouth of Muskosh River," an article by Juanita Rourke
"THE BREITHAUPTS AT THE COTTAGE,"an essay by Melissa L. Humphries,1995
SUSAN BELLINGHAM, chief librarian, Dora Lewis Rare Book Room, University of Waterloo, Waterloo, Ontario

TRANSLATION
Cognashene is an Ojibway word. Several authoritative translations of this word exist, and many more have been perpetuated orally over the years, including "the place of blueberries," "the place of porcupines," and perhaps most diplomatic of all, "the place of porcupines and blueberries." For the purposes of this book, every effort was made to find the definitive meaning of the word—to no avail. With apologies to those whose favourite translation may have been omitted, the editors settled on "the place of blueberries and porcupines."

COGNASHENE/KAIGNASHENE
Further complicating matters, there appear in the text two different spellings of the word Cognashene, the second being Kaignashene. While today only the first is in use, early on, the second was the more popular choice. The different spellings may be the result of the spotty written record of the first settlers to arrive in the area, or due to the difference in pronunciation of the early English and French settlers. In the mid-1930s, the Canadian Government demanded that one of the two spellings be permanently adopted. Since that time, the word Cognashene has been in use.